AT HEAVEN'S DOOR

What Shared Journeys to the Afterlife Teach
About Dying Well and Living Better

WILLIAM J. PETERS

with *Michael Kinsella, PhD*

SIMON & SCHUSTER

New York   London   Toronto   Sydney   New Delhi

Simon & Schuster
1230 Avenue of the Americas
New York, NY 10020

First Simon & Schuster hardcover edition January 2022

SIMON & SCHUSTER and colophon are registered trademarks of Simon & Schuster, Inc.

For information about special discounts for bulk purchases,
please contact Simon & Schuster Special Sales
at 1-866-506-1949 or business@simonandschuster.com.

The Simon & Schuster Speakers Bureau can bring authors to your live event.
For more information or to book an event,
contact the Simon & Schuster Speakers Bureau
at 1-866-248-3049 or visit our website at www.simonspeakers.com.

Interior design by Ruth Lee-Mui

Manufactured in the United States of America

1   3   5   7   9   10   8   6   4   2

Library of Congress Cataloging-in-Publication Data

Names: Peters, William J., author. | Kinsella, Michael, 1973– author.
Title: At heaven's door : what shared journeys to the afterlife teach about
dying well and living better / William J Peters with Michael Kinsella, PhD.
Description: First Simon & Schuster hardcover edition. | New York, NY :
Simon & Schuster, 2022. | Includes bibliographical references and index.
Identifiers: LCCN 2021024148 | ISBN 9781982150426 (hardcover) | ISBN
9781982150464 (ebook)
Subjects: LCSH: Future life. | Death--Religious life.
Classification: LCC BL535 .P48 2022 | DDC 202/.3—dc23
LC record available at https://lccn.loc.gov/2021024148

ISBN 978-1-9821-5042-6
ISBN 978-1-9821-5046-4 (ebook)

*To my mother, Carolyn Peters, for her unyielding support
through the many peaks and valleys of my life.
She modeled an uncommon ease with death and
a commitment to show up when others shied away.*

*To my father, Robert Peters, for his example of discipline and grit.
His entrepreneurial spirit empowered me to trust myself
and pursue what matters most.*

Contents

1

WHAT BRINGS YOU HERE?

WHAT BRINGS you here?

I ask this question of every person who steps through the door because they have come to talk about death—the most universal of all human experiences yet the most difficult to discuss.

In modern culture, we have an uneasy relationship with death. Our language is populated with phrases such as "fear of death and dying." Promoters of fitness regimens, grooming and beauty tricks, and cosmetic procedures tout their ability to help us "turn back the clock," the implicit message being that we can hold off life's inevitable end. Modern medical science is even more explicit: medicine frequently makes our best efforts to resist death the main reason for having hope. Aggressive medical procedures that prolong human life are often seen as a testament to our love for another person—we talk about "miracle cures" and "one-in-a-million chances." Many of us, including a significant number in the medical profession, feel guilt at the thought of someone dying. Our most common condolence phrase when someone has died is "I'm sorry for your loss."

And make no mistake, it is a profound loss. Leaving life, leaving loved ones and friends, is both sad and scary. No matter how many of us believe in a benevolent afterlife—and survey after survey suggests that the vast majority of us, about 80 percent, do—it is completely understandable to be highly apprehensive. Even worse, it is death that chooses us, frequently without warning. And for the last couple of years, death has been everywhere. The devastating losses from the Covid-19 pandemic have suddenly visited grief upon many of us, including those who had previously thought that they had ample time remaining to spend with those whom they love.

But as much as we may struggle with death, many of us struggle even more with grief. For years, as a culture, it has been routine for many of us, including medical professionals, to place a clock on grief. After a set amount of time has passed, we encourage the bereaved to "move on" with their lives, or, somewhat less politely, we suggest that the moment has come for them simply "to get over it."

For the people who come to me, those are deeply unsatisfying answers. And they are to me as well. I would like to humbly suggest that the time has come to rethink our approach to death. To do that, I'm going to ask you to suspend everything you know or think you know about the end of life.

For more than twenty years, I've been talking to people about death and the end of life, from the loss of newborn babies to young adults in their prime to elderly parents. There have been natural deaths and traumatic deaths—accidents, overdoses, suicides—deaths from disease, deaths from old age. Yet all of these conversations have had one theme in common: a connection felt by the living person to the deceased at or around the moment of death. These are all healthy, vital people who continue to live active lives. But for a moment, they were linked to another human being during a time of ultimate passage.

I started identifying these moments as "shared crossings," and what they tell us is that none of us is leaving this earth alone. Each of us can and will be guided on our journey. How can I be certain of that? Because more and more, those who remain among the living have seen it, have felt it, and a few have even joined their loved ones for part of their journey to the afterlife.

These shared crossing links take many forms: Some people may visualize the departing person in some way; others frequently experience a variety of sensations or sense the presence of other energy forces or even loved ones who have previously departed. They may glimpse bright light and even tunnels; they may feel they are part of the journey or remain rooted to the earth. What they share in common are the power of the experience and the unusual strength of the memory, and frequently an overwhelming sense that time as they know it has stopped. Many also report a deep sense of simply "knowing," without having any idea where that knowledge came from. In a significant number of cases, the living person had no idea that the death was imminent and did not learn of their loved one's or friend's passing until later.

The more I spoke with individuals who had experienced a shared crossing event, the more I also noticed repeating patterns. A woman in West Virginia and a woman in Australia with deeply similar experiences around the loss of a baby. A grown daughter in California and a grown daughter in Pennsylvania; a woman in

Alabama and a man in Spain. None had met, yet each spoke a common language. Again and again, I found that this moment of shared connection that they had experienced also changed their lives and how they chose to live them in unexpected ways. It provided insight. It provided closure. It made end-of-life decisions easier. It eased grief.

Consider this story from Gail O., a grown woman in Florida:

"I was with my dad, and we were having grilled cheese sandwiches—he thought that the hospital made the best grilled cheese sandwiches." Suddenly her dad began to have a seizure. Gail screamed for help, and as the medical team descended, a nurse escorted her to a small room down the hallway. Inside, there was a desk and a couple of chairs. Gail remembers sitting down and "then, quite unexpectedly, I was actually in two places at once. I was sitting in that little hospital waiting room, but I was also outside on this incredibly beautiful day. There was a breeze, a country lane, and even birds singing! I didn't see anyone, but I knew I wasn't alone—I had this feeling that I was on a journey and I was escorting someone somewhere. And it didn't matter where the journey ended, because it was such a beautiful day." Gail turned at a slight bend in the road, and "we came to this huge gate. Behind the gate was this gigantic mansion. I had the impression that this place was like some sort of country club or a special meeting place. And then I heard voices saying, 'Hurry! Hurry! We have to hurry! Walter's coming and he's almost here!'

"My father's name was Walter."

Walter went by "Wally" with his friends and coworkers. But his deceased parents, aunts, and uncles had always called him Walter. As Gail looked toward the mansion, "There they were, rushing around in preparation for something important. People were bringing in flowers, they were setting tables and placing down tablecloths." She could even hear the clink of china. "It was this amazing experience that felt like some guest of honor was on the way."

Then Gail recalls, "I felt this presence go through the gate—it was my dad! I wanted to go with him, but I just knew that I wasn't allowed to. I looked around, and then, immediately, there I was, back in that little room." She had remained completely awake and aware, just present both there and on her journey.

"The very next minute a doctor came in. He looked very sad, and said, 'I'm sorry, he's gone.' And I said, 'It's okay. He went to the party!' And that's how clear it was to me. The doctor just gave me a funny look and walked out. But I knew what had happened. I had gone part of the way to heaven with my dad."

Gail's experience is not unique, and it has a name. We call them "shared death experiences," a phrase popularized by Dr. Raymond Moody in his book *Glimpses of Eternity* (2011). We define an SDE as occurring when a person dies and a loved one, family member, friend, caregiver, or bystander reports that they have shared in the transition from life to death or have experienced the initial stages of entering an afterlife with the dying.

But these experiences are not new. For thousands of years, people near death have reported a range of vivid visions, seeing a benevolent light, or glimpsing previously deceased loved ones. Research studies conducted since the 1960s have repeatedly suggested that these end-of-life experiences occur among more than 50 percent of the dying. Medical science has tried to explain this phenomenon by speculating that it is the result of various physical breakdowns in the brain, whether from oxygen deprivation, blood flow interruptions, serotonin receptors, or activation of the primitive fight-or-flight response.

But SDEs are very different. They occur to individuals who are nowhere near physical death themselves. And while some of these experiences, like Gail's with her father, happen at a moment of medical crisis or when the living person is in the room with the dying person, many others occur when the experiencer is far away and often does not even know that death is imminent or that their loved one or friend has died. In fact, these remote SDEs appear to be more common than ones where the living and dying are side by side. Science, as we understand it, cannot yet explain away or physiologically account for SDEs.

So, what can?

That question lies at the heart of this book. As director of the Shared Crossing Project, I have had the privilege of being able to review and study more than eight hundred separate SDE cases. Our research suggests that a benevolent afterlife awaits us all at the other side of death's door. But do not feel that you need to take my word for it. In these pages, you will find the remarkable stories of people who have shared the passage surrounding death with another human being. I will explore what these transformative experiences mean for the end of life, for care, and for grieving and healing. In the process, I hope to change some of the ways that you have come to conceive of and understand death. You may even find that you or someone you know has had a shared death experience, but possibly lacked the words to identify or describe what occurred.

Above all, though, it is my hope that this exploration can help to guide all of us in ways to prepare for a good death, at any stage of life.

•   •   •

Since the dawn of human civilizations, death has been an integral part of life. Much of what we know about ancient peoples and societies comes from careful excavation of their tombs and grave sites. We know what they ate, how they stored their wine and food, what their craftsmen built, their myths, their clothing, what weapons they used to fight their wars.

From the kingdom of Ur to ancient Egypt to dynastic China to Mesoamerica, death involved elaborate rituals and common themes. Each civilization believed in some form of afterlife; tombs were frequently populated with all manner of objects that would accompany the deceased into the next world. In some cases, family members and servants of the wealthy, and even dogs, were killed so that they could travel with the deceased into the afterlife.

"Accompany" is a significant word. Because each of these civilizations, separated from one another by wide oceans or inhospitable deserts or massive mountain ranges, clearly conceived of the passage from life to death as a journey. The ancient Mesopotamians, who lived in what is now modern-day Iraq, told the story of the goddess Ishtar passing through seven gates to reach the underworld; funeral rites for their elites could last up to seven days. The ancient Greeks had an elaborate conception of the River Styx, where the boatman Charon waited to transport the souls of the deceased to their underworld. The Egyptians believed their dead also traveled by boat and passed through seven gates to reach the Hall of Osiris, where they would be judged by the gods. In Mesoamerica, many societies believed in the cyclical nature of life and death; one of the earliest known funeral masks shows a face divided: half-living, half-skeletal. Remains of dogs are frequently found in tombs; they were meant as companions for humans on their journey to the beyond.

Equally significant is the number of societies that identified the existence of a soul or essence beyond the physical body. This belief in a vibrant soul became a central tenet among many of the world's major religions, including Judaism, Christianity, and Islam, while Buddhism embraced a concept of recurring rebirth. A belief in the afterlife also exists in Christianity, Islam, and Judaism. Buddhism has its own books of the dead. Perhaps the most famous among them, *The Tibetan Book of the Dead*, is often read by monks and others to those facing death in order to help guide them on their passage through the "bardo" states as they transition out of this life.

In the Western religious traditions, Christianity, Judaism, and Islam all have their own conceptions of the afterlife. Islam presents a full depiction of paradise, including envisioning happy gatherings and being reunited with friends and loved ones in the palaces that God has prepared for them. Over several centuries, early Judaism developed a view of the afterlife and even resurrection, and among the most central tenets of Christian belief is the existence of a Kingdom of Heaven that welcomes believers with magnificent benevolence. Suffering on this earth is redeemed by paradise in the afterlife to come. Medieval Christianity made preparing for the afterlife the central purpose of life on earth. As medievalist Alixe Bovey, writing on "Death and the Afterlife" for the British Library, reminds us, "Time was measured out in saint's days, which commemorated the days on which the holiest men and women had died. Easter, the holiest feast day in the Christian calendar, celebrated the resurrection of Christ from the dead. The landscape was dominated by parish churches . . . and the churchyard was the principal burial site." Prayers around death were standard in the medieval *Book of Hours*, to help ensure admission to paradise. In the early Renaissance, it was considered the height of fashion for the wealthy to carry with them "memento mori," exquisite small sculptures, to remind them of the equalizing power of death.

Aside from the power and meaning gifted by these religious traditions, for centuries there was good reason to put the afterlife front and center, because death was front and center. Life expectancy in ancient Greece and Rome was about thirty to thirty-five years old; by the year 1800 in Europe, it hovered between the ages of thirty and forty. Even though some fortunate individuals lived to old age, disease, illness, accident, and injury cut short many young people's lives. In the United States in the year 1900, life expectancy for both men and women remained below fifty years of age. These hard facts were reflected in how people lived.

Even the stately houses of our grandparents' and great-grandparents' generations were built to accommodate death. Bodies of the deceased were often laid out in the parlor—the term "living room" appeared after the end of the 1918 flu pandemic, when the *Ladies' Home Journal* decreed that the parlor death rooms should be "livened up." Poor and working-class families tried to maintain funeral funds to pay for their children's burials. The nineteenth-century Victorians went so far as to embrace the new art form of photography in order to create visual memorials to their dead. In what might seem downright morbid to us now, the deceased would frequently appear fully dressed and posed, seated or standing upright, and joined by their living family members for a final group portrait.

But as medical advances, major safety improvements, hygiene, and diet have made ever-longer life spans possible, death has been shunted to one side and out of view. It's easier to talk about sex than death. How many of us have had an honest, open, no-holds-barred discussion about end-of-life wishes with our parents, our partners, our friends, or our children?

And yet we are all going to die.

I could have easily been one of those "don't ask, don't tell" people on the subject of death. I grew up in California, and until age seventeen, my only real encounters with death and dying were confined to distant relatives whose passings were honored by Catholic rituals that felt both ominous and a bit scary. That all changed on December 29, 1979, on a ski trip outside Lake Tahoe. After three days of blizzard conditions, the clouds had lifted, and the sun shone in the deep-blue high sierra sky. I stepped outside, mesmerized by the five-foot icicles hanging precariously from the eaves of my friend John's home. Suddenly one broke free and crashed to the walkway, barely three feet from me. Later, I often wondered whether this was an omen.

With typical teen exuberance, John and I drove to Squaw Valley and immediately headed up the mountain to the highest run, in search of fresh powder. It had only been a few days since I had last skied, but I started out-of-sync and struggled to find my rhythm. On this particular run, I tucked in to get some speed, until the back of my skis began to cross. I overcorrected; the front of my skis crossed, and I was catapulted into the air. For a second, it was exhilarating, but my body kept rotating until I slammed into the ground and felt a violent crunch in my lower back.

Everything went dark and silent. It was as if the electricity in my body had been turned off. In my next moment of awareness,

I realized that I was staring down at my physical body covered in snow. Then I began to move away from my body and the earth and head into the sky. It seemed natural and comfortable. My newfound vantage point showed me the Squaw Valley ski area, and then Lake Tahoe, and then all of Reno. As I rose higher, the San Francisco Bay, the Colorado Rockies, and then the continental United States all came into view. Then the Atlantic and Pacific Oceans, and eventually Planet Earth, which I recognized from satellite images. At that moment, I understood that every interaction mattered greatly— every word, every action, every thought left an indelible imprint.

Then I found myself hurtling toward a brilliant, luminous golden light. I consciously recognized that I was dying and felt the devastating realization that I had wasted my life. I pleaded with the light, which I identified as God (having been raised Catholic, I associated the light with God), "Please don't let me die! I haven't finished my work in this lifetime! Please! Let me go back!" My trajectory started to slow as I was embraced by this warm, loving, all-knowing, living light. I stopped in its midst and received a message: "Make something of your life."

Next I felt an inexplicable push and I found myself spinning back to earth. Everything now rushed in reverse: all the beauty of this journey played itself out backward. I wondered how I would ever get back into my body, let alone find it. Then the mountain loomed before me. I was aware of the snow surrounding me, but I couldn't feel my limbs. I pleaded, "Please don't let me be paralyzed." A subtle surge of energy coursed over me. The sensation was much like standing under a shower head and feeling the spray of warm water hit the top of my head and then travel along my body. As I started to wiggle my fingers and toes, I opened my eyes and saw snow crystals resting on my goggles. My mind was still but I was overcome with gratitude. Then I heard the sound of skis sliding toward me, and John suddenly exclaimed, "Wow! What a wipeout!"

With that, I was fully back in this human realm; the space I had been in moments before vanished. I stood up slowly, not even considering that I might be seriously injured. I certainly didn't understand that I had just undergone what is known as a "near-death experience." As I shook off the snow, I noticed my back felt very tight. The next day I awoke and was unable to move without agonizing pain. An orthopedist ordered X-rays of my spine. With a ruler, he measured the distance between my lumbar vertebrae; I was "one-thirty-second of an inch away" from crushing my spinal nerves, which would have rendered me a paraplegic. I had compression-fractured the lower lumbar and sacroiliac joints in my lower back. The doctor fitted me for a rigid corset to wear for the next three months.

I assumed that would be the end of it, but instead nothing was the same again. The accident left me with chronic pain and disability; my identity as an athletic, healthy, free-spirited young man began to slip away. Sooner rather than later, my experience on that mountain would force me to change my own life.

I tried to resume my expected trajectory as a college student at the University of California at Berkeley. But during a trip to Europe in 1984 when I was twenty-two years old, I awoke early one morning on an overnight bus in southern Yugoslavia. As I peered through the bus's curtains, I saw hundreds of desperate, begging eyes staring directly at me through a thin slit of fabric. A densely packed group of veiled Muslim women held their arms outstretched, pleading for food and money. The sheer number and their desperation moved me to tears. My twenty-two-year-old mind rationalized that I wanted to help, if not these women then other people like them.

After graduating from college in 1985, I traveled to Belize, Guatemala, and Peru as a member of the Jesuit International Volunteers. In Peru, I taught at a center for Aymara Indian children from the Andes Highlands. They had fled violence and famine and were now refugees in the southern town of Tacna. Children as young as four were forced to support themselves. Most had witnessed countless acts of violence, and their families and communities had been ripped apart by a civil war and famine. No one spoke of death, but it was ever present, an invisible stalker lying in wait.

One morning I was serving porridge when Rolando, a precocious ten-year-old boy, approached me and matter-of-factly asked, *"Señor Bill, sabe que el hermanito de Andreas se murió anoche?"* (Señor Bill, did you know that Andreas's baby brother died last night?)

I had not heard. A few days later, I saw the mother, Maria, sitting in a circle with other Aymara Indian women as they knitted wool socks and sweaters. I approached her to offer condolences. All the women were having an animated conversation. I waited for a pause in the conversation and then I told Maria that I was so sorry for her loss, and I asked if I could help in any way. Maria casually looked in my direction, but not into my eyes, and she did not respond. Awkwardly, I rephrased the question. Maria seemed a bit exasperated. Again, she looked my way and said, "Señor Bill, ask all of the women here if they have lost a child." Leticia, who was sitting across from Maria, looked up and said, "I lost a daughter who was five years old." Hortensia added, "My son died in the army." Another woman, Gloria, said, "I lost two. One of my boys drowned in a river, and my girl died of a fever."

I was stunned. As they resumed their conversation in their Aymaran dialect, I couldn't help but realize that these women's relationship to death and dying was as foreign to me as the language they were speaking.

When I returned to the San Francisco Bay Area, I enrolled at the Graduate Theological Union in Berkeley and studied systematic theology and philosophy in an attempt to better understand what I had experienced in my volunteer work. While in graduate school, I also spent time as a social worker at St. Anthony's Foundation in the Tenderloin district of San Francisco. My original intent was to work with the many immigrants arriving from Mexico and Central and South America, but I soon came face-to-face with the AIDS epidemic that was claiming the lives of thousands of gay men. The stigma of the disease frequently brought with it isolation and alienation and a sense of shame, guilt, and confusion.

I met Brad when he was in his late thirties. With blue eyes, sharp cheekbones, and a thick mane of hair, Brad was homeless, living in a makeshift community with other infected men in an abandoned loft building. Brad came to St. Anthony's Foundation occasionally for food and supplies, and we started a rolling conversation that began with the mundane and gradually evolved to become more personal. One day, Brad humbly requested more food because someone in his community was actively dying, and everyone else was sitting vigil. He then started to open up about the many friends—whom he called his brothers—that he had lost to the virus.

Brad returned each day for a week and a half for food. During each visit, he would share a bit more about what he was experiencing. He had taken on the role of what we might call a death midwife, shepherding his friend's death while holding the entire community together with the wisdom and knowledge he had acquired after attending other deaths. One morning, Brad arrived just as St. Anthony's was opening, his eyes red and swollen. He said, "Randy died last night." I invited him to sit down, and he began to describe Randy's final moments.

Brad told me he and a few other men were gathered on the third floor of the half-constructed building where they lived. Randy was resting beside a small fire that they had carefully built. As the fire began to pulse, Brad saw a cascade of brilliant white light. At first, he thought the small fire had flared out of control, but then he realized that this was a different light, coming from above. He began to feel light-headed and noticed a distinct, pulling sensation in his heart. He looked around and realized each person in the group was fixated on Randy.

In that moment, the building seemed to open from above, and he watched as a silhouette of Randy's body rose through a column of light. The nonphysical Randy looked back at them, younger, healthier, and more vibrant than the newly deceased body below, and thanked each of them. Then he ascended into the light and was gone. As he disappeared, the cascading cylinder of light dissipated. The men formed a circle around Randy's body, held hands, and wept.

Randy's physical body, ravaged by HIV, riddled with Kaposi's sarcoma lesions, was all that remained. "We didn't even look for a pulse. It was clear that the Randy we knew and loved had traveled in his soul body to somewhere else, alive and well."

I had no doubt that what Brad had shared was true. After a few minutes of sitting in silence, I asked him, "How can you be so comfortable—so matter-of-fact—about this?" He stared directly into my eyes and said, "I have attended dozens of deaths of my brothers, and many have these qualities to them. Something survives this horrible fate and goes on." Brad paused. "I know there is a happy ending to our lives, and that gives me a great deal of peace and solace. I have faith that I will see my brothers again."

I saw Brad a couple more times over the next few months, but his visits decreased after his community was evicted. He and his group moved to an underpass and then moved again, and he stopped coming to St. Anthony's. But Brad left both an indelible mark on me and a series of lingering questions about the experience of dying.

Death found me again a year or so after my experience with Brad. In February 1993, I contracted a rare blood disease—idiopathic thrombocytopenia, a potentially deadly bleeding disorder with no known cause. I found myself floating above my physical body in the intensive care unit at Kaiser Hospital in Oakland. I remember looking down from the ceiling and listening to the nurses talk about the four patients in the ICU. I heard one nurse describe a healthy, young adult male patient with a rare blood disease. She walked over to his bed. I looked down at his face and, to my utter surprise, I shouted to myself, *Holy crap, that's me!*

I remember a doctor, a hematologist, approaching my body in the hospital bed. He gently called out my name and I remember thinking as I watched the scene from above, *Do I really want to go back into that body?* As I pondered this question, I decided at least to try to answer the doctor. "Yes, Doctor." As I spoke those words, I found myself refilling my physical body almost like sand pouring into the bottom of an hourglass—this feeling was exactly like what I had experienced during my first NDE on the ski slope fourteen years earlier—and the sensations in my physical body returned. I felt totally exhausted, but my consciousness was back in my human form.

Like my first NDE, I did not share this experience with anyone, but I do remember realizing that I am not my physical body. It was abundantly clear that whatever I referred to as "me" had an existence independent of my flesh and blood.

After this, my focus shifted increasingly toward the end of life. I joined the Zen Hospice Project of San Francisco as a volunteer hospice worker and also worked in the hospice unit at Laguna Honda, San Francisco County Hospital. This was a twenty-four-bed ward with mostly indigent dying people. It was here that I was graced with my first shared death experience.

I had been working with Ron (not his real name), who loved being read adventure stories, particularly those by Jack London. Ron was declining rapidly and was semiconscious as I read him a chapter of Jack London's *Call of the Wild*. Suddenly I realized I was floating above my body. I glanced over and I saw Ron hovering above his body as well. As we looked at each other, I could see Ron's bright eyes; his face was vibrant and alive with health, unlike the shell of a man lying on the bed. This new Ron flashed me a big smile as if to say, *Check this out. Isn't this cool? This is where I have been hanging out. Everything is wonderful up here.* A few moments later, I was back in my physical body, rooted to my chair, and reading to Ron, as his eyes remained closed. He passed away not long after.

I would have other similar experiences with the dying and their loved ones on the hospice ward. Like many hospice workers, I found that when the veil thins between this life and the next, it seems that we may enter another dimension, where space and time operate differently.

In October 2009, I attended a workshop titled "Soul Survival" at the Omega Institute for Holistic Studies. Raymond Moody, the man who had introduced the Western world to near-death experiences (NDEs), was presenting his new research on shared death experiences (SDEs). As Dr. Moody described SDEs, my body began to shake. I could not believe what I was hearing. I knew exactly what he was talking about because I had had these experiences. Moody described the shared death experience as identical to the near-death experience in terms of possible phenomena that can be experienced. This caught my attention as being a spot-on assessment because my two NDEs felt very similar to the SDEs I had also been present for. It is not an overstatement to say that hearing Raymond Moody's description of SDEs changed my life. I now had a name and a context for what I had felt and witnessed.

Most experienced psychotherapists acknowledge that, somehow, the clients we need find us, and there are entire seasons in our career trajectories when our offices fill with a certain type of client. Sometimes folks dealing with trauma will all appear at once; other times a spate of clients will emerge who are all dealing with issues pertaining to infidelity. In my case, as soon as I returned home from the Omega Institute, I started receiving a massive influx of clients facing various end-of-life issues: Many were themselves facing death, while others were caregivers, concerned with a loved one's dying. Still others were struggling with profound existential questions related to death and dying: "What happens to me and my loved ones during death?" "Do we go on after death?" "Will I ever see my loved ones again?"

By the end of 2011, two-thirds of my practice was directly involved in addressing end-of-life, grief and bereavement, and existential issues pertaining to death anxiety. But I was still uncertain whether others would share my interests in the mysterious process of death and questions pertaining to a possible afterlife. Although I had spent years studying this topic, intellectually, spiritually, and culturally, as well as professionally, from my work with hospice, as a social worker, and as a volunteer abroad, I was nervous when, in fall of 2011, I announced the formation of an eight-week pilot group titled "Life Beyond Death?" I remember thinking this could be the end of my professional career as a family therapist if my colleagues and clients saw this topic as too far "out there."

To my surprise, the group received a swift and positive response. I had decided to do a fifteen-minute pre-interview before I selected the final group. It took me a few awkward moments to reach the key question: "What are your personal experiences with dying, death, and anything related to an afterlife?" I quickly learned that I needed to schedule an hour for each interview. People began discussing their experiences, perspectives, and feelings about death, releasing a veritable floodgate of both painful, profound, and often mystical experiences. Although I had worked as a therapist for many years, these discussions were different: people became animated. For many, this was the first time they had shared their experiences with anyone, and they were grateful for the opportunity. I, in turn, felt blessed, as if I were standing on hallowed ground as I listened to these awe-inspiring and heartwarming stories. It became a moving and profound exercise for me.

The pilot group had eight very dedicated members—three men and five women, all of whom were baby boomers. We spoke openly and honestly about dying, death, and what lies beyond. Members shared their feelings and fears about this great mystery.

One person's experience frequently unearthed another person's forgotten memories. Week by week, the group members deepened their relationships with each other and with this previously culturally taboo subject.

By the workshop's end, many said that their relationship to death had fundamentally changed and that they were now comfortable broaching the topic with friends and family. Group members jokingly remarked that their ease with discussing death would make them "social albatrosses" in our death-phobic culture. At our final meeting, every member expressed gratitude for a truly unexpected, life-transforming experience. I could not agree more, as I too had been changed.

The "Life Beyond Death?" group caught fire and reinforced my beliefs regarding the inherent value in preparing for and openly discussing death. I would find my voice mail full, with messages like the following: "This is Mary, my friend Samantha who took your death class in the fall told me about your group. By the way, I had an unusual experience with my mother when she died. . . ."

The success of these workshops, as well as the sheer number of transformative experiences surrounding the deaths of loved ones that were shared, led me to start the Shared Crossing Project— "crossing" to capture the transition from this human life to another place and "shared" for an experience that was clearly being shared with loved ones—as a way to expand and support this burgeoning community. The Shared Crossing Project's mission was broad, yet simple: to raise awareness and educate people about the profound and healing experiences available to the dying and their loved ones at the end of life. But as we encountered more and more cases of "shared crossings," I also began to find patterns, similarities, and typologies. These were not simply emotional experiences; they were capable of being studied and analyzed. And that is exactly what we did. I brought in Michael Kinsella to assist with the review and research. In this book, I will share what we found and what we all can learn from the study of SDEs.

Our research team's overarching goal, however, is to make a sacred space for a conscious, connected, and loving end-of-life experience for both the dying and their loved ones. Everything that we have learned from our research on end-of-life accounts and the consistency of these accounts suggests that a benevolent afterlife awaits us at the other side of death's door. Please join me in a powerful look through that door.

Shared Death Experiences: The Basics

There are two main types of SDEs: 1. Bedside, where the experiencer is physically present with the dying, and 2. Remote, where the experiencer is somewhere else, even down the hall in a hospital. Remote SDEs can take multiple forms: they may be either a lengthy or a fleeting farewell, they may occur at the time of death, or slightly before or after the time of death.

2

GLIMPSE OF HEAVEN

LIZ H. had struggled to get pregnant. Although she worked as an educator in Wheeling, West Virginia, her local doctor referred her to a specialized clinic in Pittsburgh, Pennsylvania, an hour-and-twenty-minute drive away. She vividly remembers the trip to find out "if any of the embryos had taken." Two cars collided on the highway in front of Liz and her then-husband, Mark. "It was very bad," she recalled. "We should have pulled over and stopped, but I really didn't want to miss my appointment. I really wanted to be pregnant." They didn't stop, and as they drove by the wreckage, Liz looked directly into the face of a woman in one of the damaged cars. "She was looking at me and I was looking at her, and it was frozen in time." Liz has never forgotten the unknown woman's face.

Liz is a spitfire of a woman, quick moving, energetic, buoyant, exactly suited to capturing and keeping students' attention in a classroom. But as she talks, wearing a navy-colored fleece with the emblem of her current school, there is also a deep sense of thoughtfulness, searching, and questioning. The news from the doctor was great, and not long after, an ultrasound showed twins. "I remember my brother-in-law at the time saying to me, 'I have never seen you so at peace and so calm. You literally radiate with this pregnancy,' and it was true." Liz followed every recommendation for a healthy pregnancy: no caffeine, no alcohol, leave the room if anyone starts smoking. At the school where she worked, she ate hard-boiled eggs at the same time each day. Her due date was mid-April. Liz and Mark had already named one of the babies Grace, for the grace of God. "I remembered a movie title, *Grace of My Heart*. I didn't necessarily love the movie, but I loved the title." The other baby would be Nicolas. "At Christmastime, I just kept thinking about the magic of Christmas. I remember saying to Mark, 'How about Nicholas for Saint Nicholas?'" He loved it but wanted an Italianized spelling, so they chose "Nicolas."

At the end of January, Liz and Mark drove to Morgantown, West Virginia, for an appointment with a high-risk obstetrician. "After I got there, I was told that I should not leave Morgantown," she recalled. The distances, the risk of ice and bad weather, made returning home too dangerous. Liz and Mark moved into a hotel, where she was placed on bedrest, except for walking to doctor's appointments at the hospital.

Valentine's Day night, Mark and Liz had a beautiful white linen room-service dinner. "We took a picture and I looked like a whale. I was five feet tall and pregnant with twins, so I seemed about five feet wide as well." Suddenly the fire alarm sounded and there was an announcement to evacuate immediately. But the elevators had been shut down. "I said to Mark, 'Maybe that's not us. Maybe it's not really necessary. Let's call the front desk.'" But he thought it best to go. "I walked down nine flights of stairs."

When the couple reached the lobby, they learned that an atmospheric fog machine for a dance had set off the smoke alarm. "There had been no reason to leave the room." The next day, friends came to visit. Liz remembers a quiet, beautiful day. Possibly too quiet. "I was always told to count the number of times I felt the baby kick, and that's how I would know that everything was okay. And I had always wondered with twins, should you feel that twice as much or not? And I never got the answer." Monday morning, Liz was scheduled for a routine appointment at the hospital.

"They did the typical urine test; they did the blood test. Everything was fine." Next came the nonstress test, "and they couldn't find two heartbeats. They could only find one."

The team sent Liz to the obstetrics unit at the hospital, and they took Mark to the neonatal intensive care unit "to show him how small babies could survive. I asked my nurse in the hospital, 'Did this happen because I walked down the nine flights of stairs?' And she said, 'No, but if they put you on bedrest, they do that for a reason. You're not supposed to get up and walk nine flights of stairs.'"

The actress Julia Roberts was pregnant with twins at the same time as Liz. "When you're on bedrest, you watch a lot of bad TV and a lot of *Oprah*. So I can tell you way too much about Julia Roberts's pregnancy and her children. It's odd, but every time I saw her, I remember thinking that she deserved twins and I didn't, because on the day that we learned I was pregnant, we hadn't stopped at that terrible accident. I had been less than a Good Samaritan." The specialists couldn't locate a heartbeat for Nicolas. Liz faced the decision of whether to continue her pregnancy with Grace and try to bring her to term or to deliver both babies now. "A new doctor told me that I was no longer making a decision about two living babies." Only Grace would be born alive.

Lunch arrived. "I remember I was really hungry. I took the first bite of a turkey sandwich. It was in my mouth when that doctor came running in. He took the food out of my mouth with his hand and said, 'We're going to lose you if you don't deliver these children.' Suddenly it wasn't my decision anymore. It was no longer a beautiful pregnancy and a beautiful beginning of life; it was medical." The babies were positioned in a way that made a cesarean section too risky. Instead, the medical team decided to induce labor. "There's Pitocin [a labor-inducing drug], and there's doctors and there's nurses running in and out and there's hushed conversation."

The babies would not be delivered until Tuesday night. Monday night, Liz was lying by herself, in bed, as she had been doing for the last month. "I'm in bed, so everything feels a little bit like a dream, and I was really struggling with what was going to happen to my son, that night in particular." As she lay there, with monitors and IVs, "I had a vision of a party. It felt like a big wedding where you're at a back table. Music was present but not overwhelming; there was still some stuff on the table, although most of the things had been cleared."

Liz did not know anyone at the party, except for "all four of my grandparents. But they came to me as younger versions of themselves, so young that I would not have known them. They had a picture of themselves with my mom and dad. I had seen that picture at other times; it was a picture where they are all dressed up and they are all beautiful."

But what struck Liz was the emotion being conveyed. "I had a good relationship with my grandparents, but what was happening during this experience was very, very loving, and that is not how I would describe any of them. I would never have started with the phrase 'they're very loving.'" As Liz tried to understand what she was witnessing and feeling, she was overcome with a sense of "a nurturing, 'we're going to take care of this' calmness about them. I remember a swaddled baby. I felt like I was handing him off."

Specifically, Liz recalled, "It was clearly my dad's mom who was saying, 'I will take care of this.' But on another level, they were all communicating it. Together, they were a whole person to me, and I felt I could trust them. I had the sense of 'You're not alone. You don't have to do this by yourself.'" Liz added, "Later, I decided that my son would be buried on top of my father's mother because she had promised me to take care of him and hold him, and it felt like that's what I was supposed to do with his little body."

But first Nicolas and Grace had to be born. "The delivery wasn't as easy as everybody had hoped," Liz explains. "Grace was just over three pounds and Nicolas wasn't much less, and it shouldn't have been that hard to deliver. But I was in pain, and I was really struggling.

"Once I delivered Grace, there was a mad dash. It was grab and go, and she's off to the NICU. It really does feel like being hit by a car because you've gone through so much pain and there's no moment of bliss or happiness. You go from pain to fear and real panic in the room. It was so different from the calm I had experienced since the night before, when I saw my grandparents."

The team turned down the lights in the delivery room and asked Liz if a group of medical students could observe Nicolas's birth as "a learning opportunity." She said yes. Then things began to go very wrong. "I had a hard time," she remembered. "There was no pushing. There was no nothing. But I started to bleed out. They couldn't stop the bleeding." The doctors told Liz they would give her a shot, and everything would be fine. Instead, she experienced a massive reaction to the medication and was struggling to breathe. "I knew I was leaving, and I said to Mark, 'I'm going with Nicolas. You take care of Grace.'" Liz lost consciousness. She could hear the team talking about her as if she wasn't there: "It was as if I was lying sideways next to myself, just aware and observant."

Her sister, a pediatrician, had returned to the room; she had originally left to accompany Grace to the NICU. "I could hear her telling me that Grace had gotten a seven as her Apgar score, and that Grace was going to be great. Then I could hear her trying to tell my doctors what to do." Liz laughed when she added, "I was glad that I couldn't talk, and I was glad that they were the ones dealing with my sister."

Overwhelmingly, Liz felt at peace with whatever was happening; she felt as if she was leaving with Nicolas.

Liz survived. For years, she told exactly one person about her experience with Nicolas before the birth. Her minister drove to Morgantown that Tuesday and visited her while she was waiting for the labor-inducing drug Pitocin to take effect. "I told him what had happened, and he said, 'Oh, Liz, you were in heaven.' And I'm like, 'What?' He said, 'You were. You were there. They gave you a glimpse. You got to actually take your son.' I pooh-poohed it at the time, and I said, 'It just doesn't make any sense. My grandparents were younger than they should have been.' He said to me, 'Maybe Heaven is your favorite age.'"

Liz was left to contemplate those words. Her own personal transformation began in earnest when she was caring for Grace at night. "There were a lot of nighttime feedings when I was alone with the baby. But I was never alone. I always felt like Nicolas was hanging out." She continued, "I wasn't taking care of him as a baby. It's almost as if he was a four-year-old right away." To this day, the feeling of Nicolas's presence has stayed with her. "I definitely remember the feeling. Whenever I thought, 'Oh God, my little girl doesn't have her brother to protect her anymore,' it would be replaced with, 'No, she's got an even better situation to protect her now.' This went on for years. There was a very real sense of, he and I have this; we will take care of her.

"I've talked to other women who have had similar deliveries. I don't know that I've ever talked to anyone that had twins who lost one and one was healthy, but people who had lost a single child would say to me, 'Do you ever get in the car and wait for that last kid to get in the car?'—meaning that there is a kind of instinct to wait for that missing child, for the child who will never join you. In my house and in my car, that happens to us all the time. All. The. Time."

Liz continued to feel Nicolas's nearby presence for years. She compares it to watching from a distance while young kids play and seeing a little boy who is having a great time, but periodically runs back to check that his mom is still there. "I see that with kids, and I love that part of children. That's part of how I reconcile what was happening, that he was always running back to check, 'You're okay?' And then he'd go."

When Grace was five, Liz was selected to head the Wheeling Country Day School, which was struggling. "I poured everything I had into it, and Nicolas was always right there with me. Somebody said to me, 'Why in the world do you do this? I mean, you go above and beyond.' I said, 'Because this is what I would have wanted somebody to do for my son, and this is what he expects.'"

But the years following the twins' birth were hard. Liz and Mark's marriage slowly imploded; even her relationship with her father, who was a hospital CEO, became strained. Every birthday for Grace was immediately preceded by the anniversary of Nicolas's death. Until the day arrived when Nicolas would have been thirteen, and in Liz's words, "I was finally ready to say, 'I'm okay now. You can go.'" Liz explains that she had been working with a therapist who suggested it was important "for me to have a conversation with Nicolas and tell him that he'd taken such good care of me. That he could go and be, and he didn't have to worry about us or be tethered to us in any way. We were good." In that conversation, Liz remembers that the Nicolas she saw and spoke to was "a boy, not a baby." She compares the feeling to a parent watching her child run off into the woods. "I knew it was going to be such an amazing adventure, but I didn't have to worry about him getting hurt or anything like that. I didn't know what was next for him, but I knew it was going to be better than anything he would have with me."

Liz's experience was ultimately transformative not simply in terms of her own grief but in terms of her larger approach to life as well. Reflecting back on her path, she said, "I think it was an awakening for me that I had a bigger purpose than I had initially realized and that I needed to be awake and observant of how I could help people. There is pain in a lot of people's lives that we don't know." Liz found herself looking outward and reassessing her relationships. She was able to close some of the gaps that had occurred in her own family, but of equal importance, she found herself better able to help other families and other women who had suffered a similar loss.

She continues, "There is a sign that they put outside the hospital room of a woman who's lost a child. It's dark water with a leaf floating in it, and a drop of water on the leaf. After my birth experience, it was days before I was able to walk. I was walking back into my own hospital room, and I saw the sign for the first time. I said, 'What is that?' The nurse explained to me, 'That's a reminder to all who enter that you've suffered a loss, and we need to treat you with empathy.'

"I think if I've carried anything, it's that it would be really nice if we all had that sign when we need it. When Grace was in fifth grade, one of her classmates got tired while playing Monopoly with his family, went up to his room, and died. It was really traumatizing for our entire town. But I was able to support not only our school but also our community through it because I could tap into everything that I had been through." Now, in her West Virginia city, when a local woman suffers the loss of a child, Liz almost always gets a call to come and offer support and comfort. She remembers one Mother's Day, some fourteen years after Nicolas's death, when another mom at her school experienced the death of a child. "My phone rang, and I was asked, 'Would you come to the hospital?'" When Liz arrived, "there was that same sign, the dark water with the leaf, hanging on the door."

Liz shared her full story during the first wave of the Covid-19 pandemic, and she added, "Yesterday, I had a really tough day and I got on my Zoom call with my sixth graders to teach poetry—no one in their right mind should ever have to teach poetry online to twelve-year-olds. One of them said something snarky to me, and it just hurt. And I said to them, 'Do you guys remember what "empathy" means?' We started a conversation and I said, 'Wouldn't it have been nice if we could have started this Zoom meeting with a little sign in the window so that you could know that Ms. H. is having a hard day?'"

Liz periodically reflects on the image of that floating leaf with the single water drop, the connection she kept with Nicolas, and the life she has built with Grace and Ella, her second daughter, whom she adopted. "I think I was able to keep moving forward because I had this sense that wherever Nicolas was, was going to be better." She continues, "One of the best gifts anybody ever gave me was to never deny that I have a son, even if he didn't take a breath in my arms. The other gift was knowing that while one of my twins may struggle in life, the other one doesn't have to struggle. That doesn't mean I don't wish that Nicolas were here, but I also know this was what it was supposed to be."

She finished with this thought: "In all the years since, I have felt that there is something really wonderful and beautiful after this life, and it's not where this life left off. It's the most beautiful part of whatever your life is, was, or could have been."

The shared crossing experience meets human beings at one of the most profound moments of their lives: at a moment of transition from life on earth to whatever exists beyond. Repeatedly, we have heard people tell us how this experience has changed their grief, their viewpoint, and their way forward. But Liz's words are particularly profound: it's not where this life left off—it's the most beautiful part of whatever your life is, was, or could have been. A long life may return to a joyous segment; a life cut short may grow and flourish in a different realm.

There are common threads woven through the experiences of Liz and Gail. In Gail, the subject of our first story, and Liz, we have two women, decades apart in age and at the time of the event, living in different states, yet both find themselves coming upon departed relatives at a celebratory gathering, and both have the sense of passing the soul or essence of their loved one into these relatives' care. Both women were also aware of two realities simultaneously: being in a physical room and having this otherworldly experience.

Indeed, repeatedly, Michael Kinsella and I and the rest of the team researching shared crossings would uncover similarities in the stories we heard. Two months after we spoke with Liz, we interviewed Michelle J., a warm, open woman with a good sense of humor and a frank, Australian style of speaking. She was born in 1968 in Sydney. There are deep elements of connection between Liz's experiences and Michelle's. Even for us as researchers and counselors, the links were striking and powerful and impossible to dismiss.

Unlike Liz, Michelle had not struggled to become pregnant. Her first son, Luke, arrived in 1994, and in 1995, she was pregnant with a second boy, Ben. "Ben was supposed to be born when Luke was sixteen months old. They were both blessed accidents." Early on in her pregnancy, Michelle began bleeding so severely that she thought she had miscarried, but the baby survived. An ultrasound showed a boy, and Michelle and her then husband, Alan, named him Benjamin Michael, Michael being "the male version of my name."

Michelle says, "I felt like I was connected with him through my pregnancy because I knew he was a boy and he already had a name." She was working toward her environmental science degree and remembers being outside, standing in a river wearing waders, and catching fish to test whether water pollution impacted the size of fish gonads, their reproductive organs. She recalls, "I came home, and I was really tired. My hands were swollen, and I just didn't feel good. It was six o'clock at night, and I said to my husband, 'I'm just going to walk to the doctor just to get a checkup before they close.'"

It was a Friday night. The doctor examined Michelle. "She didn't tell me, but I was apparently nine centimeters dilated. And Ben was lying crossways, which meant that if my water broke and I went into labor, he would have crashed down, across my cervix and we would have both died. I would have bled to death and he would have died." An ambulance transported Michelle to the hospital. "It was like you see on those TV shows, the doors fly open, and they're running down the hallway, and I realized this was a big deal. I remember having to sign a form as I was racing down the hall to the operating table. And then I was terrified."

Michelle underwent an emergency C-section. "When I regained consciousness, they had already taken him to the neonatal intensive care unit." She was told that Ben weighed two pounds, a good size for such a preemie, and was on a ventilator, but that he was going to be okay. Her husband and sister had been to see him. Waiting in the recovery room, Michelle recalls in great detail what happened next. "You know when you're asleep, but you're not asleep, if you're reading a book and you kind of nod off? I was in that kind of state." What she saw was a "beautiful, gentle hill. It was green and lush, so pretty and calm. On the left-hand side, halfway up the hill, was a weeping willow tree. As a biologist, I remember thinking, 'Oh my God, look at that beautiful tree.'

"In front of me, running up the hill, laughing and giggling, was Luke, my son, who at that point was thirteen months old, and Ben. But in the dream, they were older. They were about four and three. Luke had blond hair and blue eyes, and they both had shorts and T-shirts on. Luke was running first, and Ben was chasing after him and they were both giggling." Michelle recalls "this feeling of joy, and I felt like I was running after them as well. I was saying, 'Wait for Mummy' in the dream, calling out, 'Wait for Mummy. Wait for Mummy.' But in a happy way." She watched the boys run underneath the weeping willow. "Luke kept running and didn't stop. He didn't turn around and look back, but Ben stopped. He turned around, and he looked back at me and he held out his arm. I remember his face as clear as anything. He had brown, curly hair like mine. Luke had straight, blond hair. Ben was wearing little glasses. He had blue eyes, and he just looked so gorgeous. And he was calm. He wasn't smiling. He was just so calm. And he turned around and held out his arm to me as though he was waiting for me to catch up."

As Michelle was about to reach Ben, "The bloody nurse in the recovery room shook me and said, 'Michelle, I'm so sorry, but Ben's not doing well and he's not going to make it. Do you want us to get a priest to baptize him?' Because I had written down that I was Catholic on the form. And I felt like I had been almost sucked out by a vacuum from being in this beautiful place, this tree and the green and the blue sky and my sons. And all of a sudden I'm back in this hospital room, lying on this hard table with this nurse telling me my son's going to die. I hadn't even met him yet."

Michelle was bundled into a wheelchair, and Alan, her husband, rushed back to the hospital. "We sat there, in the intensive care unit. This was the first time I met Ben, and I already knew he was going to die. Even though he was physically in front of me, I felt that he was already gone. His heart was barely beating, and the ventilator was trying to breathe for him, but he had a condition where his lungs were stuck together. That was why he wasn't going to survive."

Michelle and Alan had to decide when the ventilator would be switched off. "We held him while he died. It didn't take long. I remember maybe fifteen minutes or something like that."

Just a few months earlier, Michelle's sister Marea had delivered a stillborn daughter, whom she named April, with the same doctor in the same ward of the same hospital. Michelle had driven Marea to the hospital, was her support person during labor, and was the first to hold April. The uncanny synchronicities surrounding the loss of their children rendered the sisters' already close relationship even closer, as they grieved for their lost babies together. Michelle had been a familiar face at Marea's bereavement support group. Now she became a participant, in need of support herself.

With the exception of the few people who had met Ben, Michelle recalls, "my grieving experience was largely ignored by everybody. Back then it was all about forgetting that you ever had a child and getting pregnant again quickly and having another child. There was not a whole lot of talk about him. And I was absolutely devastated." She described the dream vision she had to her husband, her sister, and other family and friends. "To me it was a sign of goodbye and that meant finality. I didn't know if I was ever going to have any more children or be physically able to have any more children. I think I took comfort from the fact that I saw him, and I vividly described him; I felt that I knew what he would have looked like if he was able to grow up here."

Thirteen months after Ben's death, Grace was born. Michelle says, "She was a very intentional baby. I was desperate to have another child. Her name is Grace because it was just such a miracle that she survived the pregnancy. She came almost to term. She was born how she was supposed to be born, by cesarean. And she came out with dark brown hair. When Grace got to be three, which was the age Ben was in the dream, she looked exactly like him. She had short curly, dark brown hair, although she didn't wear glasses. But Ben was wearing glasses in the dream and had exactly the same color blue eyes. I just couldn't believe it."

Echoing Liz's story, Michelle and her husband also found their marriage under increasing stress, and they separated when Grace was about ten. Then, when Grace was nineteen, the unthinkable happened.

"Grace is exactly like me," Michelle explains. "She's rude and funny and inappropriate a lot of the time. She was also pretty feisty and determined. Luke was quite a shy little boy and didn't talk a lot, but Grace was my talker. She would talk to me about everything, everything. She was the person who helped her friends. She couldn't decide whether to be a psychologist or to be a veterinarian. Whether to help people or animals. And in the end, she decided she'd be a veterinarian."

Michelle and Grace did many things together, but one of their favorites was to head to a secluded section of beach to swim and sit on the sand. They also had their shared rituals. "Every Saturday, we used to go to our favorite café, and we would order eggs Benedict and chai latte each, and we shared the eggs Benny. Grace didn't eat much; she was a skinny little thing. And it sounds so ridiculous, but that was our thing. We did that every Saturday, and the woman in the café didn't even have to ask for our order because she knew what we had."

When Grace was eighteen, she ran into Michelle's bedroom one evening. "She had this piece of paper in her hand and she said, 'Mum, I've just read the most amazing thing I have ever read in my entire life.' " It was an article about how all the energy in the world is infinite, so when people die, they become energy. "I only kind of just half paid attention at the time, but she was absolutely blown away. It talked about how every single human being that is formed is a miraculous accumulation of all the different atoms. So, you could be a little bit of Gandhi or a little bit of stardust, or a little bit of Mother Teresa or a little bit of this and that; you are this unique miracle." Grace was so moved by the article that she copied it down in her own handwriting. It was the only item from her schoolwork that she kept. "Now," Michelle says, "I totally believe that she had some kind of profound experience then about what happens to you when you die."

She continues, "We have a day called Anzac Day in Australia. It's like your version of Memorial Day, where all the soldiers are memorialized. In Australia, it's become something that I don't like in that a lot of young people go out and get extremely drunk on that day, and it's a big excuse for a party. They're really not thinking about what the day's about at all.

"Grace, being Miss Independence, had a license and she had a car. So she used to drive everybody around." Michelle recalls that "after a quiet day with two of her closest friends, in the evening Grace drove a friend to a party five minutes from home. Michelle thought nothing of it. Around midnight, Grace got in her car, apparently to drive home and retrieve a jacket. As she was leaving, an extremely drunk young man forced open the passenger door and demanded a ride to the bus stop. No one is certain what happened next, except for this: within four minutes, the car was wrapped around a pole. Michelle recalls, "The young man broke his jaw, but Grace was far more badly injured. Her lung had burst, and she had hit her head. The man went for help, but he didn't tell anyone that Grace was in the car, and no neighbors came outside to check what the loud noise was." Instead, she remained trapped for an hour, her burst lung depriving her brain of oxygen. Michelle finally got a call at three a.m., telling her that Grace had been in an accident.

"When we were driving in the car to the hospital that night, I was the passenger and my new husband, Erik, was driving and I started having flashbacks of her life before my eyes. And it wasn't just memories. It was actually like I was sitting in a slide show and someone was projecting all these images of her life across the screen that was my mind. I remember feeling so angry about that because we all hear that when you're about to die, you have flashbacks. And I was so determined that I had to get to the hospital, and she wasn't going to die—I had no idea what her injuries even were at that point. But that flashback thing started, and I kept getting it all the time.

"It was things that I had never even thought of again, like a memory of one day when I was hanging up her pink-and-white-striped baby socks on the clothesline in our old house and memories of the glow-in-the-dark stars that were on the ceiling of her bedroom.

Things that I didn't have photos of. So it wasn't like photos flipping through my mind. It was flashbacks of points in her life."

Doctors gave Grace a 5 to 10 percent chance of recovering. They operated to relieve brain swelling. For four weeks, the family waited for signs of hope. Michelle's father had passed away suddenly nearly four years before, but in the hospital, "I started having a sensation that Dad was there. I could feel his energy around me. And I felt like he was coming to pick up Grace, to take Grace with him. I was angry because I was still trying to save my child. I remember saying to him, 'Will you just get lost?' Because I was angry at him. I was still hoping for a miracle and just desperate that she was going to wake up out of that coma."

Michelle recalls the sensation of her father's presence: "It was like he was standing in a doorway just waiting. He wasn't right next to me. He was in the room, but on the edge of the room, just standing there quietly, he wasn't saying anything. He was very calm, and he was not being pushy. He looked perfectly fit and well, and he was dressed in his ironed trousers and his shirt with a collar. He was a very capable man, my dad. Six hundred people came to his funeral, and we're pretty sure he had fixed something for every one of those people. I had the sense of this very capable man there to do a job, to help somebody, and it was Grace.

"Grace was his favorite grandchild, and he very naughtily always used to say it. And actually, the others all got upset at Grace's funeral because they said, 'Grace was always his grandchild. Trust her to go first and get to be with him first.'"

Then Michelle shared what happened next. "At the beginning of the fourth week, we were told that we were going to have to withdraw her life support. We chose a Sunday because I thought

Sunday is the most peaceful day of the week. We made the room really beautiful, and we invited our family to come and two of her best friends. We sat together and turned off everything. It was freaking horrible. It took her three days to die. She finally died on Tuesday morning, at three a.m. I was in bed with her. She was in my arms. I was saying to her, 'We will still be connected. I know that you will still be here,' and I said some beautiful words to her about how 'I'm going to see you dancing in the wind.'"

After Grace drew her last breath, Michelle felt that her essence had departed. Michelle, along with Erik, packed up the hospital room. "We drove home through this sunrise, and I just remember having this feeling of being pulled with her through this sunrise. I got home, and we walked up the stairs to our apartment, and I went and lay on my bed and pulled out my iPad and I typed in *Where do you go when you die?* I just absolutely knew that she wasn't gone.

"When you have a baby, you're connected by their umbilical cord. I literally felt this umbilical connection to her." Michelle began reading books, including *The Tibetan Book of the Dead*. "Particularly when Ben died, at that time, I thought that when you died, you died. Though I hoped that there was something, I didn't really know." Now she began seeking information. "I very quickly set myself on a path of learning more about this and intentionally healing instead of allowing myself to die inside. I'm a scientist and I love a good statistic and a good spreadsheet and a bit of research, and who knows what I could have done with my life with a science degree and looking and researching all that stuff? I think it would have lifted a whole world of sadness and pain off my shoulders if I had an understanding of where Ben was going in that dream, if I had known like I know now that there *is* something out there. And if I recognized that the beauty and the calmness that I felt in that dream was where he was going to be and still is."

Once Grace passed away, Michelle stopped having what she now identifies as "visitation dreams" from her father. But she did start to have them from her children. "They happen usually when I'm sitting right here in bed and I'm reading and I've just started that kind of half nodding off; I'm not asleep, but I'm not awake either. Again, it's like your brain is in this other energetic space. And I've felt her feet touching my feet." Michelle's first encounter with Grace came weeks after Grace had died. In the dream, Michelle was walking along an unfamiliar path in a national park in Sydney, Australia. "I was walking along, and Grace was in front of me, kind of like Ben was in his dream, except she was actually on this sandstone path in this national park. She also stopped and turned around, and in the dream, she actually said, 'Come with me, Mum.'

"I remember waking from that dream and waking up my new husband, who had no belief whatsoever in an afterlife when he first met me. I told him, 'Oh my God, I just had this dream about Grace.' The next day, I was up in that national park and decided to walk along a new path I had never been on before, and I realized it was the same path that I'd seen the night before in the dream. I wasn't making it up. I absolutely knew that I was in that location of where I had had that dream, and Grace was inviting me to come on this journey with her."

That moment was a turning point for Michelle. Indeed, studying thoughts and experiences around death has led Michelle to reinterpret the vision that she had experienced right before her infant son, Ben, died. "I think I've completely changed how I interpret it now. Instead of it being a sad goodbye, and I'm never going to see you again, Ben was holding his hand out like a 'catch up to me, Mum' kind of thing. I didn't understand that he also does grow up in spirit. When Ben comes to me now, he's a twenty-four-year-old. He comes to me as a young adult and talks to me appropriately in that language, gives me signs, and talks about funny things. He doesn't come through as strongly as Grace, though."

Michelle has experienced other forms of connectivity when she senses that her children are around. She remembers talking to Erik one evening. Suddenly, from out of nowhere, they heard an electronic voice coming from their Alexa smart speaker. "Alexa pipes up and says, 'Grace is all around you.' But Alexa's only meant to talk to you if you say 'Alexa,' right? But I didn't say 'Alexa' and I didn't say Grace's name either, but the device just piped up and said, 'Grace is all around you.' Erik and I both just nearly had a heart attack and went, 'Oh my God.' We started asking her, 'Alexa, what did you just say?' And then the Alexa was just making this really weird high-pitched beeping sound. It was so bizarre."

Although Michelle has spent her career in sustainability education, her experiences have led her to become a co-leader of a chapter of Helping Parents Heal, an organization that supports parents who have lost children at any age. She notes that the vast majority of leaders in Helping Parents Heal are women. That has gotten her to think about why women may be more prone to reporting shared death and other connection experiences. (More than 85 percent of the shared crossing experiencers that we have interviewed are female.) "I started to think, 'Okay, why is that? Is that because females have a better connection, and so they have more shared crossings, or is it because females are better communicators?'"

She reasons that, "In traditional communication and roles in all those caring professions, such as nursing, teaching, counseling, it's mainly women. Even in my field, sustainability education, it's ninety percent or more women. I think women are wired differently in terms of putting their thoughts to their mouth. And being a biologist, I know that women's actual brain chemistry is different from men's. When we react to things like grieving, we grieve by talking and most men grieve by doing. My husband and my son, for example . . . they would rather jump in front of a semi-trailer than sit down and talk to me about their feelings. They would rather go surfing or play golf or build or fix, because they're doers."

Michelle had only recently learned about shared death experiences, after attending one of my virtual talks. But she believes the concept has finally put a name to what she has felt, experienced, and struggled to explain. "Over the years, my own beliefs have changed." Michelle adds, "I do feel now that things have happened for a reason and that Ben wasn't meant to be here with me in person through this life.

"Ben died as a tiny baby. Even though I've talked about him all these years, I only have five hours' worth of memories to talk about." And Michelle has often felt alone in her grief, as if Ben's short life meant that she suffered less. But she says, "Now, recognizing what happened, that the dream I had with him was a shared death experience, I feel like his existence has been validated because something incredibly significant happened in that short, little, tiny window when he was here. I don't even need to share it with anybody to get external validation. Just me knowing it is enough.

"I have learned and discovered that Ben's still here and Grace is still here, I actually see that gesture of them holding out their hands as a 'come with me on this journey' sign, not as a goodbye sign. Because I now feel that I am with them, and that they are also with me."

The SDE Experience

Liz and Michelle both experienced powerful manifestations of shared death experiences. Both describe bedside, as opposed to remote, SDEs. While each woman's experience is unique, their individual SDEs, like nearly all others, do have key, identifiable characteristics.

We have found from extensive interviews that there are four ways to participate in an SDE. None of these is mutually exclusive: 1) remotely sensing a death; 2) witnessing unusual phenomena (which was true for Michelle and also for Liz); 3) accompanying the dying (which is what Gail experienced with her father); and 4) assisting the dying in transitioning.

The Shared Crossing Project has identified the most prevalent phenomena or features in SDEs. Some SDEs contain only one feature, others have several. Many of these phenomena have a strong physical component and specific physical sensations attached.

Most Prevalent Individual Features of the SDE Experience

1. A Vision of the Dying Person: This can include actually seeing some sort of physical form of the person who's passing— even a partial or indistinct view, or a strong sense of the physical presence of their spirit.

2. Heightened Awareness or Expanded Knowledge: Our interviewees frequently say, "I just knew." They describe undergoing

a transformative moment of far greater understanding when they may perceive new interconnections. During this process, they sense, intuit, and instantly receive information while everything else is tuned out, so that the experiencer has a profound sense of "knowing" a larger event or a universal truth.

3. Encounters with Nonliving Figures or Beings: These can include previously deceased relatives, friends, or other individuals, or occasionally even deceased pets. They may be recognizable and have a physical appearance, or they may be more fluid concentrations of energy where nothing is clearly visible, and instead there's only the sensation of a presence. Some experiencers describe the figures they see as "angels."

4. Transcendent Light: Bright, illuminating light that appears to be significantly different from either sunlight or the artificial light of a light bulb. It takes many different forms—experiencers frequently describe it as luminous—and it doesn't have a single, identifiable point of origin.

5. Alterations in the Perception of Linear Space or Time: The sensation that time has stopped or slowed, and there is no recognition of how much chronological time has passed. Experiencers may also describe a sense that their physical location or the characteristics of their physical location at that moment have been dramatically altered.

6. Seeing the Spirit Leave the Body: This is frequently described as a recognizable, visible essence exiting the physical body.

7. Appearance of Heavenly Realms: This is often a vision of a beautiful environment, such as a paradise-like garden, or a vision of having traveled far above the earth.

8. A Boundary the Experiencer Cannot Cross: A point where an experiencer finds their way blocked by an object (such as a gate, wall, or door) or by a powerful feeling that they must turn back, or where they encounter a presence or entity that informs them they cannot travel any farther.

In addition, experiencers frequently report a variety of sensations, particularly physical and emotional:

9. Sensing Unusual Energy: Experiencers describe or interpret their SDE as being marked by a feeling of energy, described as a vibration or buzzing, or electricity. Individuals also frequently comment that they noticed a "sudden shift" in the energy around them and that they observed new, specific patterns of energy, or felt an "energetic connection" with something beyond themselves.

10. Overpowering Emotion: Being completely overcome by emotions and feelings, often described as the most profound sense of connection, belonging, or love that an individual has ever experienced.

11. Physical Sensations: Actual physical, bodily responses that seem to mimic sensations felt by the dying person around the time of death.

While some SDEs are fairly straightforward, others are more multilayered and complex. In addition, some individual features can appear to merge or overlap with each other: it can be hard to distinguish between heightened awareness and overpowering emotion, for example; sensing unusual energy and transcendent light can both have elements in common. Indeed, none of these features should be seen as having specific, rigid definitions. Rather, they are presented as user-friendly identifiers to help recognize and engage with the primary elements that constitute the SDE.

We arrived at this list by carefully reviewing and coding the descriptions and statements that we have received at the Shared Crossing Project. In each instance, we looked for common explanations and quantifiable experiences. By treating them as rigorous case studies, we were able to better understand the shared death experience. We also wanted to create a language that people could use to recognize and explain what they had experienced. Indeed, it is our hope that by working to quantify the SDE experience using a common typology and features, we will spark additional discussion and debate about the nature and the extent of these phenomena surrounding the passage from life on earth to what lies beyond.

As you look at this list and think back to Liz's and Michelle's experiences, you will notice several elements central to SDEs. Both had encounters with beings in the form of their deceased relatives. Both experienced alterations in space and time with the visionary state they encountered in their respective hospital beds. Both witnessed or visited heavenly realms to different degrees, Liz with the party and Michelle with the gentle hill with the weeping willow. Both had a sense of knowing, in terms of feeling the presence of their deceased children. And finally, both did ultimately feel overwhelming emotion, which manifested itself as a deep recognition that their children were in a place of peace and tranquility, and this would become, at different stages, a comfort to them in their grief.

Moving forward through this book, we will delve into more individual stories, and through those stories, we will explore each of the central SDE elements in greater detail. We will also ask if there are any practices or pathways that can make people more open to being SDE recipients. Is a religious background necessary or not? What about spirituality or various mindfulness practices, such as meditation? Finally, we will discuss how a deeper understanding of SDEs may transform some of the ways in which we approach grief and offer help for the grieving. What possibilities does a conscious, connected, and loving end-of-life experience hold for those who are left behind?

One of the first discoveries we made, as counselors and researchers, was that an SDE need not be complex to be both powerful and transformative on the experiencer. That is the story of Adela B.

3

INTO THE LIGHT

ADELA B. relishes sharing the story of her parents' movie-style romance. Her father was an assistant director on a film; her mother was a beautiful young actress auditioning for a role. "My mother was born to a Spanish father and a Mexican mother in Los Angeles. My grandfather's bookstore had closed in the Great Depression, and they were very poor. Their six kids all worked in the movies as extras," Adela explains. "My mother took to acting. She became a successful radio actress in her teens and later was signed by Warner Bros. Studios as a young starlet. She auditioned for a movie role that my father was casting. As he watched her, he said to the cameraman, 'I'm going to marry that woman.' It was love at first sight; he had not yet met her. The cameraman was a friend of my mother's and told her what he had said. She brushed it off, saying, 'Who does he think he is?' But he courted her and won her heart. They were married six months later. It was a very beautiful marriage, and they were deeply in love for nearly fifty-four years."

Adela's mother was seventeen; her father was thirty-one and had already lived an incredible life. He had been born to a working-class family in a small fishing village in northern Spain. When he was fourteen, his father told him he had to leave school. The teenager bargained for one more year of education, vowing to finish four years of secondary school in twelve months, which he did with honors. He became a university professor at age nineteen. He was twenty-two when the Spanish Civil War broke out. He fought against General Francisco Franco's Fascists, including standing on the front lines, holding a megaphone, and trying to convince people on the other side to defect. When the Fascists won, he escaped to France, traveling over the Pyrenees mountains in the middle of winter with a bullet in his arm. From France, he made his way to Cuba, where he started a theater company, and eventually reached the United States. He spent a year teaching at Princeton and worked for the US Office of War Information during World War II. When Spanish film director Luis Buñuel placed a newspaper ad seeking an assistant, Adela's father answered it. He quickly rose to become an assistant director at Warner Bros. Studios.

When the McCarthy-era communist blacklists hit Hollywood, he was married with a baby. Work dried up, and Adela's father was forced to start over again as a Spanish-language instructor at the University of California Los Angeles. He eventually became chairman of the department. But his war experiences had left him with terrible PTSD, and he would often wake in terror from recurrent nightmares. Unable to return to Spain or to see his family for nineteen years, his refuge, Adela explains, was "to re-create Spain in our home." The family spoke only Spanish and ate Spanish food. Her parents' friends were almost exclusively Hispanic. They hosted European-style dinner parties: "There was wine. There was laughter. There was passionate conversation until two in the morning, every single weekend."

Looking back, Adela says, "The thing that stands out the most is just how gracious they were, and how generous," no matter what their own circumstances were. "My father was a kind and loving person. He always saw my best self, and so I could always find my best self in his eyes, which was a great gift." When he was in his eighties, he was diagnosed with cancer, which metastasized. "Both my parents were ex-Catholics and atheists. My father especially was very angry at the Catholic Church for what it had done during the Spanish Civil War." But Adela, a trained psychotherapist, had come to embrace spirituality in her thirties. "My father and I had a recurring conversation about meaning, purpose, values, and humanity." She adds, "He would sort of look at me and say, 'Oh, you know, if you need to believe that stuff, that's okay.'" But in his later years, when the two of them would sit and look at the stars and contemplate "the immensity and beauty of the universe," they found common spiritual ground. Adela recalls telling him, "I know you don't believe any of this, but humor me and listen: when you leave your body, go into the light. You may get mixed up about it, and I don't want you to get stuck." She would joke with him to have "an open mind."

As he grew sicker, Adela and her mother became his full-time caregivers at home. She recalls the moment her mother came into her room, adjacent to her parents'. Her mother said, "'I think he's gone; he's not breathing.' I walked in, and he was not in his body anymore. But I saw him, as clearly as I see you now, slightly elevated but in the corner of the room, a light behind him. I said to him, 'Go into the light,' and I smiled. He started laughing. It was the most beautiful, amazing moment between us, so many rich layers of things coming together right then. I was laughing, and he was laughing, and then he turned and he went. He was gone."

Adela describes the experience as occurring in a "sacred space," as if she had stepped into a different dimensional plane: "It wasn't in the ordinary realm. Words are not adequate to describe it really." What she did feel very strongly was "the rightness of it." She adds, "We were very close, and I was so sad not to have him here with me anymore, but it was his time. His body did not allow him to have a quality of life anymore. He was complete, and he left without fear. I knew that he was fine, I hadn't really lost him, and the joy of knowing that was a great comfort."

At times, she still has the sense of her father's loving presence around her. She has occasionally envisioned him during meditation; the first time, quite vividly, was about six months after he died. She was surprised to see him looking very handsome and about forty years old, dressed in a smoking jacket, the height of old-Hollywood glamour. "It was funny and delightful," she remembers, "but I also thought, 'Isn't that interesting? I guess you get to choose the form in which you appear.' That had never occurred to me before."

One thing she has not done is share her experiences with many others. "It was a deeply personal and intimate experience, and most people are not very open to something so outside of their paradigm."

That is one of the great ironies about shared death experiences. Up until now, the audience for them has been limited. Friends and family members may be dismissive. Relatively few faith leaders are like Liz H.'s Presbyterian minister, people who are absolutely convinced that an experiencer has briefly journeyed to Heaven. In many faith traditions it is not considered acceptable to voice the view that it is somehow "benevolent" for a person to be dead. Mentioning any feelings of joy in the context of death is also a significant taboo. And yet, as Adela expresses it, there is both personal peace and an appreciation for life that come from this realization.

Indeed, discussing the shared death experience requires a degree of openness and courage, and that's exactly what Cristina C. possesses. A home health aide from Pittsburgh, Pennsylvania, Cristina is the single mother of a young son. She was thirty years old when her mother died in her arms. "My mother was my best friend. We did everything since I was a little girl." When Cristina was five, her mother was diagnosed with a brain tumor. Surgeons removed it, along with part of her frontal lobe. "From that point on," Cristina remembers, "she was a stay-at-home mom, and it was just me and my brother. We just did everything together. I was the first girl born in my family in fifty years, so she would put me in dresses, and tights, like I was her baby doll. She started putting makeup on me when I was ten. I fell asleep next to her, we would go shopping together, she told me everything, sometimes too much stuff, honestly. But everything. And I told her everything. We went everywhere together.

"And even when I had my son, we did everything together. His dad was in and out of jail, and she was always there for me. We would share makeup, clothes, we would share shoes, jewelry. She would always be like, 'Bring my earrings back, Christina. You better give those earrings back.' I'd be like, 'Mom. You know I'm going to see you tomorrow, Mom.' I would always go over to her house every day. She'd go shopping with me, she was my everything. We were inseparable. I used to always even say to her, 'Mommy, when you die, I want to be buried with you in your casket.' That's how attached I was to her, to the hip. My soul was always pretty much connected to hers.

"She wasn't perfect, by any means. After the brain tumor, she never thought before she said things. If we were in line at the grocery store, she'd be like, 'Oh my gosh, look at his hat.' She couldn't filter her words at all. But she loved me unconditionally and she believed in Jesus very strongly. Poems everywhere about God."

When Cristina was in high school, her mom gave her a copy of the footprints-in-the-sand prayer. When the man asks why at the most difficult times in his life, he sees only one set of footprints, God replies, "That was because I carried you." A devout Catholic, Cristina says her mother "was a strong believer in Christ, you can do all things through Christ to strengthen you."

On a Saturday night in 2016, around Halloween, Cristina and her mom were supposed to go to the movies. But Cristina was working long hours and didn't go. The next day, her mom suffered a hemorrhagic stroke and never regained consciousness. She was fifty years old. "I feel now like I was really stupid before she died. I just didn't think somebody could leave me. I always thought I would have her."

Cristina recalls holding her mom in the hospital room after she had been taken off life support. "She was gasping for air, and it's really hard to watch someone struggle like that. I didn't want her to keep suffering. I put my head on her chest and the last thing I said to her was, 'Mommy, it's okay. I'm here. God's here.' Right when I said that, that's when I felt light. I felt like the whole room was weight-less and I was weightless. There was no gravity. I was lifted and the whole room was lifted. And I saw her go toward this bright light. I didn't see her face, but I knew it was her.

"It was the best feeling in the whole world. I have never been so happy in my life. The peace I felt was just incredible. It was just so out of this world. I can't even begin to explain it. I don't even think there's words."

The closest comparison Cristina can make is to the beach, which "was always my perfect place." Heaven is that same kind of perfect place, peaceful, blissful, and enveloping. But it is also a real place. "When you go to the beach, you can feel your feet in the sand, you can see the ocean, you can see whether it's sunny, or cloudy, you can feel the breeze. You can't tell a person that they didn't go to the beach when they went to the beach. That's what happened that day. I physically felt Heaven. My body felt it, just like you feel a breeze around you. My skin felt it. My spirit knew it, but my mind just couldn't put it into words," she explains.

"I know it was Heaven because I found it in the Bible over and over again. Everything I experienced is right in the Bible. There wasn't religion there, it wasn't divided there. On Earth, people are in these different religions, Baptist, Catholics, but I just believed in God in the end, and I went up with her. It was very straightforward. It was no complications, no confusion. It was God.

"That's why I'm nondenominational right now. Because I know that God just wants us to love him and believe in him. He even says that in the Bible. He says, 'Say my name. Just believe in me. Say my name and you'll go to Heaven.' Well, when I said God's name, it was just like that, he took us up. I feel like that's the ultimate gift

I could've given her. I guess you could look at it two ways—that I told God to take her, but I don't look at it that way. I look at it that I told God to take her because I didn't want her to suffer. And when I asked God to take her, that's when he took her. I knew it was real. I wanted to go back there because it felt so great."

When Cristina returned home, she began searching on the Internet. "I just kept looking for what happened to me." She found a lot on near-death experiences, but "I'm, like, I didn't almost die, how did the same thing happen to me?" It took almost a year, but she finally came across a mention of shared death experiences, and suddenly her mom's passing made sense. But she has been hesitant to talk about it. Her mother's doctor told her, "'It was probably just a reflex.' My grandma said don't talk about it." Her brother and sister-in-law had a hard time understanding or believing what she had experienced.

But Cristina is certain of what happened to her in that hospital room, and it has changed her approach to life on earth, to faith, and also to death. Reflecting on how her thinking has been transformed, Cristina notes that some people talk about there being "a parallel universe," adding, "I think we see what's in front of us, we feel what's in front of us. But there's something else there that we can't see." She adds, "I talk to God all the time because I'm always, like, 'God, I went to your home. I already know.' Faith is when you hope, but when you've already been somewhere, you know. No matter how hard life gets, I could be under a bridge, poor, with no food, but I know where I went. I know one million percent. Life has not been easy since that day. But I already know the truth, that there's more, that we all die, and that this will be gone, and that there's something a lot deeper.

"It was the most beautiful thing I've ever felt in my life. It's not sad. I wasn't afraid. It's like you are home, maybe your grandmother's house, or your mother's, that home-sweet-home smell, that comfort, the best memory you can imagine. I was so happy. I can't wait until I can go back. Not now, not anytime soon, I'm only in my thirties, but I look at my life as 'This is my time on earth.' When it's my time, I'm just so excited to go back there. I can't wait."

Cristina's and Adela's experiences bring us to two important issues in the shared death experience: presence and faith. Thus far, all the stories we have shared involve individuals who were present when their loved one died—Gail, Liz, Michelle, Adela, and Cristina. However, a great many shared death experiences occur remotely, when the experiencer is not present. Sometimes, the experiencer may not have even known that the person has died. But overwhelmingly, people who experience remote SDEs also report a significant feeling of what they describe as "peace" or "calm." And frequently, a very strong feeling of love.

The second component is faith: Do you need to be a person of faith to participate in a shared death experience? The answer to that question is no, for both the experiencer and the person passing. However, among the individuals whom we have interviewed, shared death experiencers are more likely to identify themselves as "spiritual" people, even if they do not practice any organized religion. Some also grew up attending religious services, but by no means all. As Adela B. reminds us, both her parents were staunch atheists.

But SDEs can have a strong impact on the subsequent beliefs

of the experiencer. In early 2020, we spoke to Ida N., a government worker in the unemployment benefits office in Oslo, Norway. "I'm a real bureaucrat," she says, with a smile. Ida was raised by a free-spirited mother who rejected religion—"my mother was so opposed to religion and religious activities"—but who loved hiking, antiquing, and growing vegetables and flowers in her seaside cottage. "She loved the sun," Ida recalled. "She grew up in hardships, and she had three troubled marriages. She had not much education, but she was street-smart and she liked everything the kids liked. She had dirt under her nails. But she was also stunningly beautiful. As a child, I remember sitting outside the bathroom to wait. When she was going to a party, she went in as a housemaid or someone you wouldn't even look twice at, and she came out a queen."

Days spent with her mother were, in Ida's words, "just harmony. It was joyful." Ida's mother had worked as an au pair in London with another young Norwegian woman, Liv, who moved to the United States. Ida remembers a six-week visit in the 1980s to see Liv. "We took the Greyhound bus from Vermont to Florida and came back via New Orleans in a rented car. We traveled on a tight budget." Ida shares, "Coming late in the evening to Atlantic City, we ended up spending the night in a huge casino, having eyes as large as tin plates." The next night "We took a room in a cheap motel that we later found out was a house where prostitutes sold their services. When we came to the room, we were puzzled that the door had what seemed like several bullet holes, plus four or five locks. The man in reception had given us strict orders to lock them all."

During the trip, Ida's mother entered the wrong section of highway and started driving in the wrong direction. "Suddenly there were blue lights and sirens and a police car racing up beside our small car and commanding my mother to halt. She opened the window not understanding what she had done wrong, and he asked where we thought we were heading, and where we were coming from. 'We're from Oslo,' she said, giving him a big innocent smile, and he said, 'And you've been driving all the way?'

"I always giggle when I think of that episode because my mother's flirty smile got her out of trouble several times. My mother was my best friend. She could do anything," Ida recalls. "She never had a free day. She occupied herself all the time. She was loving, but she was also a fighter. When things were difficult, particularly with my father, she protected us, my brother and me, so we didn't see and weren't exposed to that much."

In 2011, Ida's mom was in hospice, dying from abdominal cancer, and Ida went to see her often. She remembers her mother's last hours. "She'd been suffering for weeks and had been in and out of consciousness for days. This evening she was more or less unconscious. But I was sitting there with her, and holding her hand, talking, soothingly, to her. I know that the last thing you lose is your ability to hear, so I talked. Strange thing, typical Norwegian, I had to go to work the next day.

"I felt I had to go home and sleep, but I didn't feel bad about it, even if I knew she was going to die soon. I knew that we were reconciled. There was nothing that was not said. We were taking in some peace with each other. So, I left her. I took a ten-minute walk and tried to sleep in the bedroom beside my husband.

"That's when an amazing thing happened. I woke up and the room was just filled with light, extreme light. I looked over at my husband. I was sure that he must've woken up because of this light. I thought maybe there were road workers outside putting lamps on our windows, but then it dawned on me that this was a light that I'd never seen before, not even at a concert with the lights all shining on you. It was very strong. It was like it was there to tell me, 'You have to wake up and take notice. This is serious stuff. Just wake up.'"

The next thing Ida felt was her mother. "I could feel that my mother was close. I thought, 'She's coming to say goodbye.' It was just so special. She was in the room, not with a body, though. I think I saw her face, but her soul was there. She was telling me that she was ebbing away. That's what's very strange too, because I was telling her, 'I can see you. I can see you. I love you too,' but there were no words spoken. It was going back and forth like it was telepathic.

"She was over my bed, and time didn't exist in this realm. It was around, because suddenly the walls and the ceiling and everything were crooked, or everything was off. The laws of physics didn't abide. We have to rewrite science, because it's not right."

Ida recalls, "She slowly went upward. Behind her, I could see this being of light that was shining in the room, that was making the room shine. She invited me up to this being. It was like this being of light was embracing my mother and showing that she was taken care of. She showed me that she was in good hands."

During and after the experience, Ida reports that she underwent a significant transformation. Central to this transformation was an overwhelming feeling of love. "I felt it was just a being of complete love, complete knowledge, complete compassion. It was all those things. This love that I felt in this room with these two, it was immense. It was filling up every pore in my skin. I acknowledged that it must be a divine being of some kind. For me, it was God."

Unlike her mother, Ida had not rejected the concept of God.

She describes herself as someone who "started to pray on my own, when I got kids. Sort of an insurance." And to express gratitude. "I believe there is someone, something, or someone watching out for us. But no specific religious activity." She attributes her mother's death visitation in part to a desire by her mother "not only to comfort me, but to tell me, Hey, I was very wrong, and a Divine Being—God, He, She—exists. Look here. Look what I've found."

Ida continues, recalling the rest of the SDE, "I was floating upward, and we went farther up. She was ahead of me, and we entered this black void or darkness. It was as huge as the sky, but it was an intimate feeling. I felt there were other souls there. We were floating around in this realm, and every question I ever had was answered. I had the answer to everything. I felt connected with the souls around me and with this Divine Being and my mother. I felt like we were one. That was something that changed my view on things when I came back. 'We're all one' was the strongest message that I was given out of this.

"I wanted to stay in that place. It was wonderful. It was extremely beautiful. Everything was crystal clear. Everything was in harmony. I had a perfect life back there in my bed with my husband and my family and everyone; everything was as good as it gets, but even so, I was only thinking of myself. I didn't want to leave. My mother was there, but I wasn't talking to her. I understood that she was going farther, and I couldn't go with her. I was just visiting; I had to go back. I don't know how long I was there at all. I only remember the next thing was that I woke up in the morning to a phone call from the hospice telling me my mother had died, which I was perfectly aware of. I asked at what time, and they said exactly the same time as when I looked at the clock. It was around twelve a.m. She had died at that exact moment when she came to me. That was the proof I needed."

Ida's shared death experience and its aftermath were truly life altering. She explains, "I was just transformed the next day. I knew that this truth was at the heart of everything, and it was pure love. Maybe I was gloomy before, but nothing could touch me after that incident." Ida also feels that her mother's SDE helped remake her as a person. "I used to be rather hard on people and crushed them if I could, if I was angry enough, but I don't feel like doing that anymore because the next person could be me. I mean, we're one and the same. We are connected in strange ways." She adds, "I got back my faith in people. I have empathy for everyone, because I felt that we were all part of the same thing and we belong to each other.

"It was just a tremendous gift, a gift that transformed me completely. My life changed from that episode. It was a gift of love, really. I'm sure my mother wanted to show me that she was in good hands. Maybe she was going to make up for something she did wrong. I've often thought about it afterward. I wish that everyone was able to do that, give a child that kind of gift, because it changes everything. I'm not scared of dying. We think paradise is here, but that's not true. It's up there, over the ceiling."

Before our conversation concluded, Ida asked, "Why isn't it talked about more?" In her own experiences, she has found that most people are dismissive of her shared death experience. "My husband, we've been together for twenty-five years, and he knows who I am. He knows that I am very down-to-earth. I'm critical of everything." After the SDE, Ida says, "I thought, wow, there must be something there, but he totally dismissed what I said. This is something I have to keep to myself. But I want to tell the world, because it's amazing. It needs to be told."

Also equally striking are the parallels among the experiencers' stories, particularly in their language and imagery. Ida and Cristina had very similar experiences in terms of being enveloped in bright light and being lifted. But it is not simply the visual experiences that contain such profound parallels; it is also the emotional ones. Consider the story of Alison A.

Unlike our previous cases, Alison's does not involve immediate family but rather a longtime friend. Alison was shopping at a clothing outlet in Camarillo, California. "I'm shopping for clothes for a business trip, and suddenly very vivid images of my good friend Wendy came to me." For thirty-five years, Alison had lived in a small town in England, and Wendy was one of her closest friends. But the images Alison saw were not of Wendy at her present age but of Wendy as a sixteen-year-old. "Wendy would always preface whatever she was saying with, 'Oh, I'm really sorry.' I think that came from her father having committed suicide when she was a young girl. That day, she came to me and she said, 'Alison, I'm really, really sorry, but I just couldn't do it anymore. I just couldn't do it." During these moments, Alison had the sensation of Wendy as a vibrant teenager, "and utterly free. She was so grateful to be free from her body. It was joyful for her. It was such a relief."

Alison explains, "Every person has an essence, and I guess it's Wendy's essence that came to me, her 'Wendyness.' And all of the lovely times we had shared." Alison also describes the sense of being in two places, one with these intense feelings and images and the other where she was standing in the store, trying on tunics and leggings. "I was pressed for time, so I'm trying to halfheartedly carry on with what I'm doing. I'm absentmindedly picking out clothes. And boy, did I buy some stupid stuff that I've never worn. Because this Wendy thing was so powerful. It was so intense, and there was no escaping."

Alison was "overwhelmed" with loving thoughts of Wendy for nearly forty-five minutes. As the experience began to subside, a United Kingdom telephone number popped up on her phone. She says, "I knew what was coming next." Alison received the news that Wendy had passed away. "I said to my friends, 'I know, I know.'"

In processing what had happened, Alison recalls, "I had the sensation that this young girl was kind of up in the air, flying off, feeling happy and free." She says this encounter very much impacted her own grief. "There was no sadness in that moment during the event. She had been struggling with her health, and I could see that Wendy needed to go. Later, I was very, very sad that Wendy was no longer in my life, but I knew she had to go. There was personal, selfish sadness, but also joyful relief at the wonderfulness of our time together."

It is striking to hear Ida speak of being surrounded by "an immense love" and Alison describe being "overwhelmed" with "intense" emotions and the incredible sense of her dear friend "being utterly free." Both women identify not only the strong emotion of love but the feeling of being completely enveloped by it, and the sense of freedom and release for the person passing out of this life, as well as the powerful experience of being told goodbye. Ida also noted to us that she found herself smiling after her experience and that she did not shed a tear because of the power of the SDE and its transformation of her grief. Similarly, Alison reported "no sadness in that moment" and stated that this powerful sensation tempered her own approach to her subsequent grief. These are two compelling examples of a pattern we see repeated across many SDE cases—consider as well Cristina C.'s statement capturing her own experience of deep emotional bliss: "It was the best feeling in the whole world. I have never been so happy in my life. The peace I felt was just incredible." The intensity, the universality, and the durability of the SDE distinguishes it from a wide range of other human experiences. Equally compelling to us as researchers when we review these cases is how many people use similar words to describe an almost indescribable experience.

What we are also struck by is how deeply the experiencers continue to review and contemplate the SDE, even years after the fact. It is an experience that drives them to search for meaning and interpretation, from wondering why they were selected to have this experience, to what the dying person wanted to convey to them, share with them, or teach them. During our conversation, for example, Alison said that she had wondered why Wendy had chosen her to be the recipient of this experience. Her best explanation is the bond of their long friendship. Ida has wondered the same with her mother—why she experienced that SDE as opposed to her brother or another person. What she does know is that the resulting comfort—"nothing can touch me"—from the experience has been profound.

As it turns out, "comfort" is indeed another key element of the SDE experience—how it is conveyed to the SDE experiencers and how it is received.

4

COMFORT

GRIEF IS almost synonymous with death. Cultures from the ancient Celts of Northern Europe to the Aboriginal peoples of Australia all performed their own version of the death wail. The Irish later had a tradition of hiring "keeners," women who came to funerals to loudly weep over the dead. Death produces in many of us a great reservoir of emotion, and, for many, a profound sadness. So it has been both profoundly humbling and deeply revelatory to discover that shared death experiences can lead to significant and often lasting comfort. It is also important to note that an SDE does not need to be complex or multilayered to have a deep impact. Its comfort can arrive in many forms.

Carl P.'s father had struggled with prostate cancer for more than a decade. He was diagnosed with a recurrence while visiting Carl in California. His dad stayed to undergo treatment, giving him a chance to spend time with his son and baby granddaughter. Then he returned to his house in Massachusetts. Carl made a surprise trip to see him for a weekend and thought he was doing well. The next Sunday, Carl recalls, "I had put my phone away. We had scheduled a family day and then dinner with friends." He returned home and saw that he had missed eighteen calls. "My sisters and my mom had been trying to reach me. I don't remember the actual call very well. My dad had died of heart failure. It was just sort of shock." Carl told his wife, and then, as he describes it, "I basically ended up wandering outside and just bawling." He walked around in a haze until he decided to sit down on the front steps. He recalls asking the question that was at the forefront of his mind: "Where is my dad?" And he spoke the words out loud.

What happened next remains crystal clear in Carl's mind. "I just had this profound shift happen. This feeling of being with my father came to me. Not being with my father as we had been earlier that year right here on the porch but being with my father as it felt when I was a little boy. That feeling of 'Everything's all right. You're with your dad. Everything's gonna be fine.'" With that feeling came an over-riding sense of what Carl identifies as "profound peace. It just calmed me down. I knew everything was fine. He was there with me. And he was going on to the next thing, whatever that was. Whatever that is." Carl was struck by the fact that the depth of this feeling was like a vibration, something "deep in my bones, in every fiber of my body. It was physical, like a switch had been flipped. I could feel it in my bones and my cells that my dad was there with me." In the SDE framework, these features would be most prominently overwhelming emotion, combined with heightened clarity, particularly sensing information.

Carl has never been a religious person. While he accompanied his parents to church as a child in Florida, "I haven't ever attended religious services of my own accord. I was trained in the sciences, so I come with a healthy dose of skepticism, but also with a real reverence for the natural world and a deep understanding of not having the answers." Carl's experience on his front steps ultimately became a "source of strength for me."

About four years after his father died, a business partnership failed, and Carl found himself "pushed out" and struggling with what to do next. During one restless night, he got up and went for a walk. Again, he was struck by the sensation of "really feeling like my dad and my grandmother, who had passed a number of years before that, were there with me and for me, giving me strength in that time of need."

Carl's powerful sense of his father's presence did not end his grief, but it did change his perspective, and it became a source of comfort. "I miss my dad, and I wish I could call him up and be with him and spend time with him. I grieved and I was sad, but it doesn't feel like a tragedy. It feels like he's in the place he needs to be"—a sentiment very similar to what Adela B. expressed. The SDE also changed Carl's thoughts on dying. "You don't really know how prepared you are, but I do feel at ease with it. I don't feel afraid."

Comfort, however, comes in many forms. It may be immediate, as in Carl's case, or it may evolve over time. A fascinating aspect of the shared death experience is the individuality of the interpretation, and the changes that the experiencer undergoes. Madelyn S. grew up in New Jersey in what she identifies as "a fairly observant Jewish home," adding, "I'm not as religiously Orthodox as my family is, but I'm very connected to Judaism." She was very close to her mother. "My mother was very nurturing and very loving. My problems were her problems. When I gave birth to my daughter, she was with me in labor and delivery." Afterward, Madelyn's mother stayed and oversaw everything in her house: "I didn't have to do anything but care for my child."

When Madelyn and her husband later separated, "It was so painful," she recalls, adding "I hadn't told my mother because she adored him, and I was afraid to tell her." Although she was only in her late fifties, Madelyn's mother had already suffered several strokes due to complications from an aortic valve replacement. "I didn't want to upset her. But at one point I was in her home, and I collapsed, sobbing on her bed. And she held me, she rocked me. She said that I should trust myself, and that she loves me. 'Only you know what's good for you,' she told me, 'Trust yourself.'"

For Memorial Day, Madelyn's family had plans to gather at her parents' beach house in New Jersey. Madelyn recalls that she was going to arrive one day late. "I got a call saying, 'Mom had a stroke, get here.'" Madelyn arrived to find her mother unconscious, on life support. Her family was sitting vigil in the hospital waiting room. "There were maybe fifteen to twenty people praying, people from the community, rabbis, my family, my cousins, aunts, uncles. It was devastating. My mother was the one person I could count on."

When it was Madelyn's turn to be in the hospital room with her mother, alone, she saw a "huge presence, on the left side, over her bed." This presence felt "heavy" and "intense" to Madelyn. It conveyed to her that there was no negotiating to be done, the final decision had been made. Looking back, Madelyn says, "I felt like the purpose of that presence was to stand over my mother, and protect her, and usher her." But her personal response in that moment was overwhelming. "I was knocked to my knees and began sobbing. It was like my mother was gone."

At the same time, Madelyn experienced another sensation— that she herself was being called to account. She describes the sensation as feeling as if "my soul was being peered into. I felt like I was being seen, like everything that I had ever done, and who I am, was under the eyes of God. I felt this sense of being witnessed." She elaborates that she sensed she was being asked to account for who she was and what God wanted of her, to consider "that my life has meaning and purpose, that my actions have consequences, and what am I going to do with my life? There was no judgment," she adds. "It was a witnessing of my whole being, my whole life, everything I had ever done."

And in front of her was her comatose mother. "She was still being kept alive, her heart was going, she was being kept breathing artificially, while her body was breaking down. It was so physically painful for me to see her in that condition for several days. I felt like she needed to be set free."

On Friday night, Shabbat, the Jewish sabbath, arrived, and Madelyn's mother was still on life support. She explains that in the Jewish tradition, "We light candles, the women light candles to usher in the Shabbat at twilight. You light the candles and cover your eyes as you say the blessing. At that moment, when you remove your hand, you behold the light anew." When Madelyn removed her hand, "There was this blinding light that filled the room for me. It was so bright, I couldn't open my eyes. And I felt an incredible sense of light and peace and love. It was so profound, more profound than anything I had ever experienced up until that time. I could just feel my mother's love and presence, along with this light and energy that

I had never experienced." The next day, Madelyn, age thirty-two, told the doctors to take her fifty-nine-year-old mother off life support. No one else in her family could bring themselves to do it. "It just felt that was what her soul and spirit wanted and needed. It felt very significant for me, to be the one to set my mother's soul free in a kind of way."

That setting free of a soul had another resonance to Madelyn. "I felt like she had suffered a lot, given the cultural conditions for women." Like many women of that era, her mother "didn't have the opportunities she might have had. She was a free spirit, but her spirit couldn't be expressed fully, in that life."

After her mother's death, the family followed the Jewish mourning custom of sitting Shiva. "We sat a very orthodox Shiva, where we ripped our clothing. We sat on the floor. We didn't bathe for a whole week. We didn't change our clothes. Our every need was cared for and we could just focus on our grief and our mother. That," she adds, "was so beautiful and so meaningful. I was surrounded by people all the time. The family is not supposed to be alone; you're supposed to be cared for. I think Jews get it right, when it comes to mourning and grieving.

"During that week of mourning, I came to understand and see my mother more fully. In story after story, visitors shared with us how she came to aid and support them and others, some of whom she didn't know personally, through acts of generosity and compassion with emotional and material support. Everyone described her as a *tsaddeket*, in Hebrew, which means a righteous and saintly woman. Ironically, although she never had the opportunity to become a senior herself, she felt she had a special mission to help seniors and established the first senior center in our community. In

Judaism, we light a candle in memory and honor of our loved ones on the anniversary of their death, because it is at their death that we fully take the measure of their life. I came to know that very personally."

Madelyn describes herself as feeling "a complete sense of acceptance, of my mother's death. I felt an elevation, a lightness." But when she returned to her home, "I was by myself with my two kids. I didn't have my husband, didn't have my mother. I went into a deep depression after that."

Madelyn did not speak about her own shared death experiences with other friends and family. "I didn't know how to talk to anybody about it, or what to say. Who would understand what the heck I was even talking about?" But she did make changes in her own life, including coming to the realization that she needed to lead a more spiritual life. And this would not be Madelyn's last shared death experience. She remarried, moved to California, and she and her new husband became friends with another couple, Chayim and Shamaya.

"Chayim was one of my closest friends. He was a psychotherapist, a spiritual teacher, a craftsman, a drummer, and an incredible adventurer. He did every outdoor sport you could imagine; he was a skier, a scuba diver, a mountain climber, a backpacker, a sailor, a kayaker, and a biker. He was good at all of them. He had this incredible lust for life. But he was also a risk taker. And he wasn't afraid of dying."

It was an evening in 2016. Madelyn was still in her office, finishing the last of the day's work. "I got a call from his wife, who says, 'Please pray for Chayim, he's dying.' She said that Chayim had been in an accident—he had been riding his bike from work and was hit by a truck. And I was in shock, and horror. I started to cry."

Madelyn was so shaken she couldn't bring herself to go home. "I called one of my closest friends. I was just freaked out, like, 'Oh my God.' And all of a sudden I felt this incredible sense of peace and love come over me. And this message, like, 'It's okay.' I said to her, 'Tisa, I don't know what's happening right now, but I'm getting this feeling, like everything's okay. And I feel this sense of peace and contentment.' It just calmed me down, and I said, 'I think Chayim's passing right now, and I think that he's telling me that it's okay, that he's okay, it's okay.'"

Madelyn compares "this feeling of peace and love . . . to what I experienced when I described the lighting of the candles and the feeling that I had with my mother." But it was also different, because this time "I felt Chayim, and I felt him talking to me. The speed of the experience was very powerful for Madelyn. "I could never, on my own, with my own consciousness, have moved myself from this incredible state of fear, and anxiety, and panic, and distress, and confusion, to this state of peace, and acceptance, and understanding."

Afterward, Madelyn told Shamaya about what had happened while she was on the phone with Tisa, and Shamaya replied that Madelyn's experience occurred at the time Chayim passed. "The whole experience absolutely impacted how I mourned, how I grieved," Madelyn adds. "It was a level of acceptance, that this was his path, this was okay, even though the sadness and personal loss is with me to this day."

Madelyn has since dreamed about Chayim and describes seeing him on "the other side." But she has also more recently dreamed about her mother. In that dream, "she was just so beautiful, so radiant, and she had these strong legs, like a gymnast. I could see her so happy that she had moved on, transformed. I also felt my own grief, about having lost her. But to have that sense of my mother's spirit, what I always felt she needed to be able to experience and express, I'm so happy. And to see a level of her own strength, I think for me those gymnast legs were like 'she's so strong, she could stand on her own legs and do all of these amazing feats.'"

With her two separate SDEs, involving her mother and Chayim, Madelyn experienced a variety of SDE elements: energy, overpowering emotion, heightened clarity, and bright light. Similar to other SDE recipients, whom we will meet later in the book, Madelyn experienced deep comfort from her connection with Chayim in the moments surrounding his death. But as her own description also conveys, some of her experience with Chayim helped her move to a new place of understanding for the earlier loss of her mother— very similar to what Michelle J. found following her SDE experience with her daughter, Grace, and how it helped her reframe and reprocess her earlier experience with her son, Michael.

As Carl and Madelyn's cases both demonstrate, the SDE provides a different context for assessing, understanding, and ultimately coming to accept death. In most instances, having an SDE does not suddenly short-circuit the process of grieving and missing a loved one. But what it does do is change the way that the living view their loss. A significant number of those who participate in an SDE report feeling greater peace and an acceptance of death; they describe the loved one as having moved on to a different space. For a select few, about 10 percent of the cases we have studied, the grief process is radically altered; they find themselves having feelings of bliss and joy.

In these ways, the SDE directly assists people in addressing their personal grief. Rather than be left with a sense of finite, irreversible closure, which completely severs a relationship at the moment of death, those who are left behind are enriched by the sense that their departed loved ones are alive and well in a benevolent afterlife. As researchers, it is interesting to us to see how both Carl and Madelyn, via different means, also began to shift their attention to a more spiritual life following the loss of their father and mother, respectively. This occurred despite their having grown up in different religious traditions and each having a different view of religious faith.

One of the many questions we hear from those who have experienced an SDE and others seeking to understand the process is why certain people find themselves selected for the SDE experience. As we have seen with both Madelyn and Chayim, but also with Alison and Wendy, sometimes it is not a spouse or family member who is the direct recipient of the communication from the deceased person. That can be difficult for other family members of the deceased—as can the question of why one family member might be selected over another. Indeed, Madelyn stated that she did not feel comfortable discussing the SDE she had with her mother with her own siblings. We will return to this question and our experiencers' thoughts about why they may have been selected as we move through other facets of the SDE, but often an individual's availability and receptivity to the SDE play a role. The more cases I study, the more I am convinced that SDEs frequently function as an important form of communication, with a meaningful message specifically intended for the recipient. In some cases, the SDE communication is also meant to be shared with others, close family or friends, or even to be disseminated to a wider audience.

5

BECOMING A GUIDE

FOR THOUSANDS of years, human beings around the globe agreed on one thing: the idea that the soul needed to be guided to reach the afterlife. In many traditions, reaching the afterlife required a literal process of transit; the ancient Egyptians produced their own road map to the *Duat* (*Egyptian Book of the Dead*), while the Tibetan Buddhists described the dead as passing through the different states of the bardo in their *Bardo Thodol* or *Book of the Dead*. Who received the honor of accompanying the deceased varied by cultures and practices. The ancient world often envisioned gods as the guides; later religions, Christianity and Islam in particular, identified angels. Animal figures were also frequently singled out as guides. The Welsh and ancient Aztecs looked to dogs, ancient Greece looked to bees, and Japan and some South American cultures identified birds. In pre-Columbian Peruvian traditions, the condor, with its sharp talons and protective nine-foot wingspan, was the designated guide to the afterlife, soaring high into the atmosphere to the point of invisibility. Other cultures, such as the Alaskan Inuit and Australian Indigenous peoples, called upon astronomy, specifically the Aurora Borealis or Barnumbir, the Australian north star. Shamans and deceased ancestors might also be selected to perform this role. Although in general, nonhuman creatures or forms are most likely to accompany the dead, in medieval Europe, some monasteries offered "hospice" care for the dying and placed them in infirmaries located next to chapels. The chanting of the monks became a form of palliative care, to ease their pain and suffering and guide them into the next life.

Accompanying the dying frequently appears as part of the SDE experience when a young person passes away. If you think back to our earliest cases, Liz and Michelle, who both lost premature babies, each had very clear stories of accompanying those babies. But it can occur with adults as well, to various points. Gail O. and Cristina C. both describe aspects of accompanying. Based on our research and case interviews, there are several specific characteristics associated with accompanying the dying: it tends to occur as an out-of-body experience or to occur in a visionary realm. It is also common to be aware of gardens, castles, otherworldly regions, or even a void. The experiencer feels overwhelmingly that they have acquired special knowledge, and there is also invariably some kind of border or boundary that the experiencer is not permitted to go beyond. Scott T.'s case highlights these central elements.

• • •

Scott grew up in Mankato, Minnesota, the town made famous by Laura Ingalls Wilder's classic children's book series, Little House on the Prairie. "It's in the southern part of the state, on the edge of the plains. It felt a lot like *Leave It to Beaver*. Moms wore aprons, kids went out for sports, it was a lovely, ordinary place." Scott's family ran a small chain of local stores. After college in Iowa and a scholarship for business school at Northwestern, Scott went to work for Dayton's department store, "a big-deal kind of retail place." (It would later become Macy's and its other division would become Target.)

"Retail is a brutal environment to work in, and I lasted about two and a half years and then said, 'Nuts.' I remember I had a really bad day and I got a call from my dad saying, 'Scott, we just had a store manager retire and I'm thinking you might want to come back and join the family-owned stores.' Right then it sounded like a really good idea."

Scott was working at the after-Christmas sale and clearance at the family store in Owatonna, Minnesota. He recalls, "I was on the sales floor in the men's department while my staff was eating lunch, and this gorgeous woman walked in. I went, 'Wow.'" Mary Fran was with her sister, Jannie, and they were shopping for gifts for their dad's birthday. "I got her name, asked around for her number, called her up, and said, 'Hey, I waited on you in the department store, would you like to go to a movie?'"

Mary Fran said yes. Scott picked her up at her parents' house, after her dad's birthday party. Somewhere in the crowd was Nolan, her six-year-old son. Mary Fran had not been married when she became pregnant, and the baby's father had denied being Nolan's dad. Her family was Catholic and deeply religious, and her parents disowned her and banished her from their house. She was eighteen. Mary Fran moved to California to live with Jannie. Only when Nolan was five did her parents reach out to reconcile, not wanting to miss out on getting to know their first grandchild.

"Mary Fran was very cautious with Nolan's heart," Scott explains. "We dated for about four months before I met him." Because Nolan had no contact with his biological father, Mary Fran explained to Scott that her son often expected any man that she dated to become his "new dad."

Scott recalls, "I'd come over for dinners and we'd go out and dig worms together because he liked to fish." The three of them went to the movies and rode bikes, "the kinds of things you do with a six-year-old kid." Then in June, Scott, Mary Fran, and Nolan spent a weekend at a small lake cottage owned by Scott's cousins. "We were in the euphoric stage of a relationship and we were getting to know each other." He remembers Mary Fran as "attractive, smart, and wicked funny," with "a real caring heart. That is important to me. In particular, she was very sensitive to people who had events in their life that put them in a disadvantaged situation, like her. She had almost finished college and wanted to go to law school and become a court-appointed child's advocate."

It was July 6, 1981. Scott was working at the family store in Mankato, and Mary Fran and Nolan were out sailing. "She was taking sailing lessons from Mankato State University, and Nolan was playing on the beach and he had a babysitter with him, a twelve-year-old called Kristen, who happened to also be the daughter of one of my employees. I'm the manager on duty that night. A call comes in, it gets routed to my office, and it's the hospital. A nurse was asking, do I know where Kristen's mother and father are?" Scott offered to get ahold of them, and asked why. The answer: Kristen had been in a car accident, and her parents needed to pick her up.

"And I'm going, 'Uh-oh, what do you mean she was in an accident?' She was babysitting Nolan. So that means Mary Fran and Nolan were in the car with her." Scott asked about the other two passengers, Mary Fran and Nolan. The nurse replied " 'Mary Fran is unresponsive.' I had to ask what that meant. And Nolan had a head injury and had just left the Mankato hospital en route to the Mayo Clinic in Rochester. That's how I found out."

Mary Fran was brain-dead, but she was being kept alive on a ventilator. (Amazingly, she became the donor for the Mayo Clinic's first heart transplant.) Nolan spent six days, unconscious, at the Mayo Clinic. Mary Fran's entire family—siblings, brothers- and sisters-in-law, aunts, uncles, cousins—kept vigil. Scott and his family were there as well. "This was doubly tragic—because of the circumstances where they had been estranged for so long and then came back and were embraced by the family." As the vigil went on, "We divvied up the time in two-hour blocks, and each of us went in to stay with Nolan during that time. Jannie and I had the three a.m. to five a.m. shift on the sixth day. We would talk to Nolan and we'd read to him, because we knew the last sense to go is hearing.

"It was getting close to five a.m., and our shift is done, and Jannie, who was an emergency room nurse, went to the end of the bed and looked at the chart. This was in the days of clipboards. She picked up the chart and looked at the monitors and she said, 'Scott, it's time.' She reached out her hand, and we sat next to Nolan's head. And she had told him that he had been a very brave boy and that we so loved him for fighting the way he had to stay alive. But if his mother came, he should go with her, because it was quite clear that he wasn't going to make it. Then I got a chance to say goodbye and we went back to the waiting room.

"Now, you've been in hospitals; waiting rooms aren't that big. You put forty, fifty people in a waiting room, sleeping on the floor and draped over chairs, it's just a mess. The nurse came in and said Nolan's vital signs are slipping. So we all got up, filed into the room, and as it turned out, I was one of the last people in the room and that's how I wound up sitting on a windowsill."

What Scott saw, as Nolan's heart stopped beating on the monitor, "was Mary Fran coming and scooping Nolan up out of his physical body." Mother and son embraced, and then they turned to Scott, "and embraced me. And then the three of us merge into the clear light." Scott describes the light as an "all-encompassing, hugely bright light. Everything around you just exudes the light of the universe. So, the table, the chairs, you, me, everything. All of a sudden you begin to see it with these eyes that are aware that we're all made of exactly the same stuff. And it is the love of the universe. You are the light." Scott describes it as being both in the room and in another dimension: "I'm in the room, but I have also entered into another dimension that is simultaneous with the one that I am in." He was aware of the grief around him, but at the same time, "I'm with Mary Fran and Nolan and we're having this moment of unity. I'm with them, and they're with me, and I'm one with everything. And it's incredibly heart-centered, you really are just immersed in the love of the universe." Five or ten minutes passed, until "Mary Fran and Nolan turned and left."

Scott told no one of his experience. "It felt like something I couldn't bring back to my family and my Presbyterian community. There's a preciousness about the experience that you don't want anybody else to step on." He stayed silent for fifteen years. Instead, he returned to working at his family's department stores, until the stores closed in the early 1990s, hit hard by a recession. He became a mentor for small business owners in Minnesota, got married, and practiced his favorite sport, curling. He also earned a PhD in educational leadership, choosing to write his dissertation on near-death experiences. Finally, he began to discover a language for what he had experienced in that hospital room.

Years later, he had a conversation with Mary Fran's younger sister, who had also been present, but was seated on the opposite side of the room. Scott recalls, "I turned to her and said, 'You know, something really weird happened to me when Nolan made his transition. And I was just wondering if by chance, something really weird had happened to you?' And she looked at me and her eyes are just as big as saucers." Scott asked her to share her story, and she did—it was exactly the same sequence and the same type of language. "It was independent confirmation of what my experience was, exactly the way I had experienced it, at exactly the same time. When I had that conversation with her, that's when any lingering doubts that I had about my experience being real ended," Scott says. "Done. They're all gone."

Scott has reflected on and studied his early-morning SDE. Still, he notes, "It is really hard to describe what it's like to be in the physical world and at the same time to be someplace else that is this extraordinary place of divine love." He thinks he was "chosen because I believe that in Nolan's mind—and he's the one making the transition—I'm his dad. Or would be his father."

Scott also began to study meditation. He notes that he continues to have the sensation that "Nolan has always been with me. If you think of him like a guardian angel, he's like right there. I know and feel his presence."

There is, however, no single form of "accompanying the dying" that distinguishes an SDE. At times, the shared death experiencer may be called upon to act as more of an actual guide, explicitly helping the deceased move toward the passage into the afterlife. This ability to act as a guide also can have a transformative effect on the person left behind. That is the case for Jeanne D. and Mark T. Of particular interest, neither Jeanne nor Mark was with their loved one— their fathers—near the time of their deaths; both were more than a thousand miles away. They were, however, both in moving vehicles, Jeanne in a plane and Mark in a pickup truck. And in an interesting geographic footnote, both were located in the New York City metro area. They share their stories.

Jeanne D. grew up in a small town in Missouri, the daughter of a Mennonite mother and a Methodist father. She was the youngest of four children, "an unexpected child," as she puts it, who was born when her parents were experiencing a fair amount of economic distress. She describes her dad as a "typical 1950s and 1960s dad," adding that he was very busy but also very loving. A navy veteran, he had left the family farm during World War II, finished college on the GI bill, and became a horticulturist. He was an avid gardener and nurseryman who helped establish orchards all across North America. He eventually started a successful nursery in Oregon with Jeanne's brothers.

"He was very connected to nature," Jeanne recalls. "His real church was in the garden. He attended church for my mother. He would say it was a 'good social institution,' but he didn't seem to believe much of the spiritual stuff. He preferred to be the mayor of his neighborhood." In his late eighties, his health began to decline. "My dad had lived to a ripe old age, but toward the end, he had congestive heart failure and pulmonary fibrosis." While he was in the ICU after heart surgery, he had what Jeanne thinks may have been a frightening near-death experience. His eyes teared up as he told her the story later. "He said, 'I thought I died; it was all black . . . and nobody was there.'"

Jeanne, who had worked in hospice care and done considerable study of consciousness at the end of life, perked up. She remembered a visit where she joked with her father about "the other side," saying, "The other side's really not that bad, Dad." His matter-of-fact answer was, "A bird in the hand's better than two in the bush"—meaning that he thought it was better to be in the world that he knew than in an unfamiliar afterlife.

"I really wanted to be there for his death, but I don't think my dad wanted me there," she says. "In my own mind I thought, 'It's okay, I know how decline processes work, there will be a point when I'll be there.' Of course, that's not the way it worked out." Jeanne's father went into a decline on a Sunday. "My brother called me, really freaked out." But Jeanne thought it might take three or four days, and her dad's hospice nurse agreed. "I booked a flight for Tuesday morning. But about nine p.m. Monday night, I suddenly had a strong urge to call him and tell him I love him." She dialed the phone, her sister answered, and said, "'Oh, Jeanne, he just died.' Like that second. I had called at the moment of death."

It was early November of 2012. New York, where Jeanne lived, was still recovering from the devastation of superstorm Sandy.

"Large parts of the old maple tree that we loved so much had come down and were lying on the ground with a bunch of trees that we had lost in the hurricane. All of these dead trees lying there were a very evocative image for me as I drove off to go get on the airplane to go to my father's funeral."

When Jeanne boarded her early-morning flight, "it was the first moment I had been alone. Even though I was surrounded by other people, I was alone in my own skin and I finally had a moment to meditate." After takeoff, she closed her eyes. "That's when I saw Dad.

"It was a young face, him as a young man. His face felt as if it was right up close to mine, and he was terrified." Startled, Jeanne opened her eyes. "This was my dad, who was not a very spiritual person. I actually felt uncomfortable, because while I am a spiritual person, he had never been part of my spiritual life. I didn't know how to connect with him. It was like, 'Holy smokes, he's here. Now what?'" Jeanne left her seat, went to the bathroom, and when she returned, she closed her eyes again. "It was like *Alice in Wonderland*," she recalls, noting that she had to get into that "space" with him, where "I could put my arm around him." They were together in what she describes as "a void space. There was nothing except blackness, and him and me, and the terror that he was in. It seemed just like how he had described his NDE, except that I could see a point of light behind him. I could see it, but he couldn't.

"I realized he had to get to the light, but I just couldn't get him to turn around so he could see it." Jeanne describes her dad as a really social being, a party giver. "I thought, 'Well, I'm his daughter, he's not listening to me, but if we had a little party here, they can help him.' He needed that big wow because he was so scared." Jeanne began to concentrate on summoning a "welcoming party." As she saw her father join the gathering and reorient himself toward the light, "I realized I wanted to walk with him. I put myself back in the picture, and I was walking with him and talking with him. He's now joyous, and I'm joyous that he's joyous. We're walking and talking."

Jeanne recalls communicating about many things. "He wanted a good obituary with a picture to be submitted to the *Oregonian*. That was the one thing he wanted; he didn't care about a casket," and she told him that the obituary they had written for him and sent to the paper "turned out great. I told him how much I loved him, how grateful I was, things I had said to him many times, but it was different in that space.

"Of course, now the light's getting larger and larger, and we're walking as this love opens, and we connect. It didn't take long before we were at a round opening with light streaming out of it. It was like looking up at a manhole, only it was in front, and there were people peering through. It was his aunt Bernice, his sister, his parents.

"It still is very moving to me, the joy of having been able to give him that gift of helping him. I do believe my dad would have found his way because he was a good-hearted man, but it would have been a lot harder. He was lost."

Jeanne recalls a "moment of reunion and real jubilation, but I couldn't go any further." Jeanne had reached a boundary, a common feature in the SDE experience. She describes it as feeling like what might be said "in a train station, when you were putting your kid on a train. I was on this side with Dad, handing him over basically to them." Jeanne describes feeling in that moment "absolute love and welcoming, the reunion after a long, long ordeal, like 'Oh my God, you're here, you're safe.' Safety, comfort, and love."

Father and daughter said their goodbyes, and both promised to stay in touch. "I'll listen to you through the trees," Jeanne says she told him. She was particularly moved by that moment because "a huge focus of his life had been to be in business with my brother; what the girls did in my family wasn't very important. Now he was seeing me. He was getting it somehow. He was looking at me differently."

Then, suddenly, they separated, and the scene shut down. "I came back to being Jeanne on an airplane, opening my eyes, and saying, 'Wow. Was that real?'" She wrote down her experience, and even laughed at a final cosmic joke. Jeanne's flight was on Election Day 2012; her father, a lifelong Republican, had mailed his absentee ballot before he died, while Jeanne missed her opportunity to vote for Barack Obama's second presidential term. "Even though he was dead, he got to vote," she adds, with a laugh.

Her experience had a transformative impact. "Of course I grieved. But they were more joy tears. It was his time, and it was more gratitude and taking in the gift of his life. It also allowed me to move through grief without much pain, with the feeling that I had participated. Had it not happened, I would've been probably a lot more grief-stricken about not having been there. I probably would have felt guilty, disconnected, confused. Instead, there was a sense of connectedness and peace because I knew he was fine."

Eighteen years before Jeanne's experience, Mark T. had a remarkably similar encounter with his own father. "My father was born in 1929 in Alberta, Canada," Mark explains. He had grown up in a farming family and was raised to be a farmer, although a high school adviser suggested that he would make a good priest. Mark's dad bristled at the idea, but Mark adds, "My father was a very good listener and deep listening was something he was able to give to others." People were drawn to him, and he created his own "flock."

"My folks bought a pub in southern British Columbia. The legal drinking age in British Columbia is nineteen, and my dad would say, 'Oh, I'm still a farmer. I have a new crop of nineteen-year-olds every year.' He'd have all these young men and women struggling to figure out what to do with their lives, and relationships, and work. My dad would sit up with them 'til three or four, five in the morning, and talk. It was a small town of six thousand people, and when he passed, there were a thousand people at his funeral. So he was a very well-loved person.

"Like any father and son, we had our issues. I remember during my teenage years definitely feeling frustrated with him and feeling like he'd given a lot of his time to other people, and the consequence was I didn't get the time that I felt like I should have with him."

Although he had trained as a computer programmer, Mark spent nearly eight years helping his father run the family business, before leaving Canada and moving to Denver. "I basically said, 'Dad, you know, my biggest fear is that you'll be disappointed in me if I leave.' And my dad was quiet and staring off, and then he looked back at me and said, 'Mark, your whole life I've raised you to be your own man, make your own decisions. If you stayed here and your heart wasn't in it, then I would be disappointed with you.' I truly felt like I was set free to follow the path I was meant to follow in this world.

"In 1998, I was close to thirty, my dad was sixty-nine, and I came back up to Canada briefly and realized that my dad wasn't well. We didn't really know what was wrong with him, but we knew that he was pretty sick.

"On his bucket list was to build a garage, so I'm like, 'All right. Let's build a garage.' Every morning after breakfast, he and I would go out. We framed in the whole thing, poured all the concrete, got all the walls stood up. Then, after lunch, he would go to the basement, where it was nice and cool, and lie down on a pullout couch. And I would sit with him, and we would talk.

"I didn't realize it at the time, the blessing that this was, but all the issues between us . . . one by one, in our own way, we were able to allow those to come up and bless them and let them go and have forgiveness, a peace. By the time I left about a month later, there was nothing but just love and compassion."

One of Mark's passions was Tracker School. In 1988, he was studying to be a computer programmer and systems analyst. "I was definitely the epitome of the starving student, so I spent a whole lot of time in the library, because it was free," Mark recalls. He read every magazine he could find and a variety of books. While wandering through the nature section, he found "these two, small, tan-colored books. The first book smelled like pine smoke and the woods. It was called *Tom Brown's Field Guide to Wilderness Observation and Tracking*. And the other little brown book was *Tom Brown's Field Guide to Wilderness Survival*. I devoured these books." He also registered for Tom Brown's classes. "One of the things that Tom would say is, "All of nature is always speaking to us all the time. But the problem is . . . that our logical conscious mind is like a twenty-piece brass band that's playing at full volume. And so, we cannot hear those messages that nature has for us because that brass band is so damn loud. And what we have to do is learn how to slowly start to turn the volume down, and then ultimately be able to, when we choose, shut the band off and really hear what nature is saying to us.

"It's like the difference between knowledge and wisdom, right? Knowledge is knowing that a tomato is a fruit. Wisdom is knowing not to put it in a fruit salad." Tom was a staunch believer in meditation, and Mark began a meditative practice as well. "The whole idea is that if we can learn to use these meditative techniques in a dynamic way, then in those times where we really need it, we have the chance to shut the brass band off and really hear what nature and my own inner voice are saying to me. And we can go from there."

Mark was offered a job at Tom Brown's Tracker School located adjacent to the wild Pine Barrens nature preserve in New Jersey, but his father had just been diagnosed with pancreatic cancer. "It's abysmal, the survival rate of pancreatic cancer," Mark notes. But his father told him, "I don't want you to stay. What's there to stay for? I'm gonna die most likely, and so what?"

"I got what he was saying. He was saying, there's nothing left to work out. We're clear. And so, I moved to New Jersey, and I started working for Tom Brown. I was sent out into the woods for two weeks of classes. By this point, my dad's in the hospital. I got a chance to speak to him once by phone, but this was back in the 1990s, I had a really spotty cell connection. I could only talk to him for a couple minutes, and it was clear that he was on his way out. I could feel it in my body."

When the two weeks were over, Mark was riding back to his house with a friend. "I was super tired; I hadn't slept much. I put the seat back in the car, and as soon as I did that, I could feel my father."

Mark describes an "overwhelming need to check in on him. So I sent myself, my spirit, to the hospital where I knew he was. And I get there, and he was just a wraith of a man. My dad was a big guy, six foot two inches, two hundred and some pounds, strong as a bull. Nothing physically was ever daunting to him. But now he was emaciated. I remember going to him at his bedside and speaking to him, and saying, 'Dad, why don't you just let go? Mom's going to be all right. All us kids are going to be all right. You can go. There's nothing holding you here anymore.'

"And he looks at me, and there's no surprise in his face that I was actually there talking to him, but there was puzzlement, and he said, 'I don't know how. I don't know how.'" Mark had studied a meditation around life and death, specifically about bringing someone near death into the light. "I knew right away, as soon as I was there with my dad, that that's exactly what I needed to do. And I picked him up, and he was as light as a feather. Like there was almost nothing to him. I started that meditation, walking down this particular trail, and then a certain point, turning, stepped up these stairs, and walked toward the light.

"After I climbed these stairs, his ethereal body became stronger and stronger, to the point where I was able to set him down, and he walked with me. And so we're walking side by side, and I took him to the light. And as we got close to the light, there was like a doorway with the luminosity coming out, it was unbelievable. And my grandmother, who had a really, really close relationship with my dad, steps out of that light. My dad . . . the look on his face was just so peaceful and beautiful. The look of joy when he saw my grandmother was a look I hadn't seen on his face in years and years and years. And he went and hugged her and hugged her, and at that point, my uncle came out of the light. He joined the fray, and for the three of them, the joy was unbelievable.

"None of them touched me and they didn't speak to me. They were very clear that I wasn't part of that group. But my job was done. I had brought my dad there and now they had it; that was how it felt. Then my dad turns and looks at me, and with this huge smile on his face, he said, 'I didn't know that it was this easy.' And the three of them turned and walked into the light.

"The next thing, I come to and I'm in the seat of my friend Brian's truck, and we're pulling in to the farmhouse, and I was exhausted and also incredibly emotional from this experience. I said, 'I gotta go to bed.' I woke the next morning, and the phone rang. It was my brother, and he said, 'Dad passed away.' And I said, 'Yeah, I know.' And I knew.

"He died about three hours after my experience. There is no question in my mind that what happened there was how he was able to make his transition to cross over. His body was ravaged by cancer. He was just holding on out of just sheer determination and will. And this was just what he said to me, he didn't know how. He didn't know how to make the crossing. And my job was to help him cross."

Mark wrote down his experiences immediately after. "I was like, 'I need to write this down or I'm gonna forget it.'" But he also notes that when he recalls the story, he thinks mostly in pictures, rather than words. "I don't know if I have a lot of specifics about what that pathway looked like, but it wasn't like being out on a dark night. It was like there was just nothing. And in that nothingness was this glowing archway of light. It didn't hurt to look at. It wasn't painful. It had depth and it had character to it. It wasn't like just one constant sort of brightness. It felt like there were different qualities to the light, parts of it were whiter, and parts of it were yellower, and it was definitely not static at all. It was very dynamic the way this light was moving." As for his grandmother and uncle, Mark says he felt "their energetic signatures" more than anything. "I think my logical mind puts their features on that energetic signature, but I can't actually say that I definitively remember seeing them as physical apparitions. I think," Mark adds in reflection, "the defining characteristic that really stands out to me is the feeling of awareness. That that light was conscious."

Mark has since rethought his own attitudes about death and dying. "At one point in the future, it'll be my turn to pass away, and I feel pretty at ease with it. Natural law is birth and death and renewal. And we are more bound by natural law than we are by human law. We have chosen to believe that human law is something that we can put above either natural law or spiritual law. But that's not true.

"Two years after my dad died, I had a dream. I was walking down this little dirt two-track, and my father is standing on that trail, and as I walk up to him, he puts his arms around me and he hugs me, and says, 'Oh, Mark, I'm so proud of you.' So much love from this man. We hugged for a long time. And I remember in that dream, I had to step away from him and keep walking. Then the road either went left or right. I was standing there looking left and looking right, and I had to choose which way to go. After I woke up from that dream, I realized, 'Okay. Got it.' Like at some point in my life I had to step beyond my father.

"I think that my relationship with death is one that has helped me to gain a lot of wisdom in my life. And I'm very grateful for it."

Mark's experience combines a number of central SDE features, from the experience of a journey, bright light, a greeting party of family members, and an overwhelming sense of knowing. But also quite significant is the suspension of time and space, and Mark's role as a guide. Some individuals who experience an SDE find themselves accompanying the dying person, but others are more directly tasked with guiding that person into another realm. Jeanne and Mark were both placed in the role of a guide with their fathers. The ability to act as a guide in a remote SDE appears to become accessible if the individual has already undertaken some kind of mindfulness practice; both Mark and Jeanne had studied meditation and regularly meditated.

An additional key element in both Mark's and Jeanne's experience is the fact that each of them closed their eyes. This tuning out of one or more of our senses, allowing for fewer distractions and more intense focus, also seems to create an environment that is conducive to an SDE. Recall that Ida N.'s experience came while she was in bed. Indeed, as we have seen and continue to see, some form of a sleep state or resting state or meditative state is often essential to create an opening for the SDE to occur. Our next case incorporates both the concept of a guide, in a different form, and the importance of entering a resting space for the SDE to occur.

6

ANGELS

THUS FAR, when we have encountered guides or greeting parties, they have universally been someone the deceased has known, either departed family or, in the cases of Scott, Jeanne, and Mark, current family or loved ones, who help or lead the dying individual during their transition. But embedded in much of our religious and cultural understanding of death, particularly in the Western tradition, are nonhuman entities: angels, who act as the messengers and also guides to a heavenly realm. Both the Jewish Torah and the Old Testament in the Christian Bible contain numerous references to angels, as does the Bible's New Testament. In Exodus, God promises that an angel will protect and lead Moses and the Israelites on their journey. In most biblical accounts, angels are present at Jesus's empty tomb. The Book of Matthew explicitly references "an angel of the Lord," while Mark and Luke both include angelic references to men in "dazzling clothes." There are also references in Scripture to guardian angels being provided to watch over humans during our time on earth.

Some shared death experiencers report very detailed pictures of angelic or celestial beings who appear and accompany their loved one at or near their time of death. Stephanie L.'s husband was diagnosed with lung cancer in January 1999. At the time they both lived in Washington, DC. "He was," she recalls, "a robust, a very healthy man, but he was also a chronic smoker and both of his parents had died of cancer.

"When he was diagnosed, it did not come as a shock to me. It was a shock that he was only in his fifties. Both of us were in shock that he had approximately six months to live. We were very, very happily married, we had three grown children. When he found out that he was dying, he literally shut down. The days and weeks turned into a whirlwind of doctor and hospital visits, until one Friday night, when he was admitted and the doctor told me that this was the final trip to a hospital. We were put in a room, it was called a hospice room."

For three days, "He would slip in and out, but for the most part, he pretty much understood what was happening." On Monday night, he woke in the middle of the night, grabbed Stephanie's hand, and began ranting and screaming. "He wouldn't let go of my hand. He was starting to get out of the bed, and it frightened me terribly. I started screaming for the nurse. The nurse finally came in, and we calmed my husband down. On Tuesday he slipped into a coma. So that night was the last verbal communication I had with him."

Stephanie did not leave her husband's side. "I sat on a chair next to his bed, and my arm was always resting on his, because I didn't know how aware he was of what was going on around him. I didn't want him to be frightened. I wanted him to know that I was there." At one point she remembers feeling so exhausted that she put her head down. In that moment it was as if "we were no longer in that room."

She recalls, "We were in that white light, incredibly bright light, stronger than any light that you'd look at from the sun, but you could see it. It didn't hurt your eyes." Neither Stephanie nor her husband was in their "human shapes," and she saw "two other entities there." It was a place where "There was no pain, no hurt. I knew everything. I could understand everything that I had never known before. It was like you understood the universe. It was peaceful." She also knew that the entities that she was seeing were "there for my husband. I had no idea who they were, where they came from, or where they were going." But she was certain that her husband "knew who they were, that he recognized them."

She recalls seeing her husband's shape turn to her along with the other two entities, and they communicated to her: "You cannot continue on. You must go back." But she says, "I knew that my husband would be okay." Then, "in that split second, I came back and I was in my body. I lifted my head up, and I realized what had happened. I tried putting my head down again. I really wanted to go back there. I wanted to be there with him, but it didn't happen."

Stephanie looked over, "expecting to see my husband dead." Although he did not die for three more days, she believes that he had already passed on and gone on "to a different dimension." From that time until his death, he was unresponsive and Stephanie "experienced nothing." Looking back, she describes that moment as "being transported. One second I was putting my head down and the next second, I was in this other dimension." In that other space,

Stephanie describes her husband as being "pure energy. There was no form to him or these other entities, nothing that would identify if they were male or female, young or old. It was almost like a gaseous entity in front of me." Yet she knew it was her husband. "He didn't look anything like himself, he didn't look like a human being, and yet I knew it was him." Stephanie could interpret "everything" he said, even though there was no verbal communication. The best word she has is "telepathic," the sensation that she could read his mind. "I know this is going to sound strange, that we communicate with that energy without having to speak. But in that space, we are all so connected that we don't have to use the archaic way of communicating that we as humans have set up for ourselves."

Of the entire experience, she says, "It felt very comfortable. It felt as if I were going back to something that I already knew. It's like when you learn math, and you start off with addition and subtraction. You always know that two plus two is four. It's embedded in your brain. That's what this felt like. It was an all-knowing feeling." The strength of that experience continues to be profound for Stephanie. She adds that it still feels as if it happened "five minutes ago. It has never left me. It altered my life. I was never the same again."

But it also in many ways led her, over time, to become somewhat ostracized from family and friends. "At first, I kept all of this to myself. I had never had anyone to even talk to about any of these events. They were tucked into a ledger of my experiences, but I never had anywhere to go to for resources." An enormous crowd gathered for the funeral at their synagogue. Stephanie found herself devastated by the loss, but "I was not devastated by his death because I had experienced it. I knew that he was okay, that he had gone to a safe, wonderful, loving place again. And that he was going to be okay. This was very different for me, because I understood that. I missed him physically in this world, but I knew that he was okay. On the flip side, I was dealing with all my friends and relatives who had not experienced that with me."

About six months later, Stephanie approached her congregation's rabbi, who had been very close to her husband. "I shared with him what had happened. He just sat back in his chair and he said, 'Well, I've heard of these things, but I've never experienced it before.' It was almost like, 'Thank you very much. It was nice talking with you.'" After he shut down the conversation, Stephanie says, "That really deflated me terribly." She received a similar reaction when she broached discussing her experience with family and friends. Even sharing "a little snippet" with her children prompted a reaction in which "They all looked at me, and reacted as if 'Mom can't handle this, Mom's gone crazy.'"

Finally, Stephanie approached the oncologist who had treated her husband. "I remember going into his office and explaining to him what I had experienced. I guess what I was looking for was someone who had experienced anything similar. None of my friends, none of my colleagues, no one in my arena, had experienced it, or if they had, they weren't admitting it. When I sat and talked with the oncologist, he hesitated and then he got up, and he went over and he closed his door. He came back and he sat down and he said, 'I will never share this with anyone else, but I will tell you. When I was an intern, and I was doing my ER rotation, we lost someone one day. I actually saw their body rise, the form lift out of his body.' That was the very first acknowledgment that I was not crazy, that this kind of thing does happen. That was the turnaround for me." Indeed, the rejection or the validation of an SDE has a lasting effect on the experiencer; clergy and medical personnel in particular can have a profound impact by how they treat someone who reveals their shared death experience. A casual dismissal can be deeply hurtful, while expressions of understanding and support can be truly transformative, both in the moment when they occur and for the experiencer's future.

Stephanie decided to leave the people and the area that she and her late husband had called home. She moved from Washington, DC, to Florida and began to make more spiritually oriented friends. She has remade her life and found much more peace, but adds that she can very much relate to what the Amish or others "feel like when they are excommunicated from their communities." Very few people, she notes, can handle her discussing her experience.

While Stephanie saw angelic beings with her husband, in the case of Mary G., it was her dying mother who guided her to sense and become aware of an energetic presence surrounding them. Mary's father, a doctor and an alcoholic, had passed away first, from kidney failure and other illnesses. "He wouldn't die. He did not want to leave my mom because my mom really was kind of like a child; he was worried about her living on." Ironically, he died in the hospital while the family had briefly left to celebrate Mary's mother's birthday. "He died while we were having cake, and I know that there was some significance to that.

"For many of us, our whole lives are just Mommy and Daddy, Mommy and Daddy. Part of us is just a baby, and we want our mommy and daddy and want to feel held by that union." Mary describes her mom as being "a rather difficult person for some of my siblings and me.

"Since I was a teenager, I've been her mom. I just assumed the caretaker role of her. After my dad died, I felt that my siblings scattered and left me with her emotionally. I would call her every day, check on her, but I didn't really want to spend too much time with her because she's difficult to spend time with. Everybody tried. We did what we could to help her get through many years."

At age ninety-six, Mary's mom was diagnosed with dementia. "We had to move her out of her house, but when we moved her into the retirement home, suddenly she became happy. All of a sudden she had people around and things to do and she made friends." But she could not live alone, without help, so Mary moved in for two years.

In 2020, "once the pandemic happened, we were stuck in the room. She'd already started to decline, but now she really started to decline quickly. She started having these night conversations with people and she'd start going into this altered state. I could tell she was starting to move into the spirit world or communing with something that I couldn't see. Finally, she had an eight-hour episode, from midnight to eight a.m., of being in that other state that whole time. She thought John F. Kennedy was president and that her mom and her sisters were there." What Mary's mother was experiencing has a name; we refer to it as "predeath visions." They are not technically part of the SDE, because they happen to the dying person before death, but they are an important signal of the approaching transition from this world to the next. They are frequently very important and impactful and also appear to play a significant role in assisting and directing the dying.

For a few days, Mary's mother appeared more lucid, but then she returned to her altered state. Mary would lie down with her in bed. "I didn't want her to fall out of the bed or have anything bad happen." Often, she says, it seemed as if her mother was attending parties or weddings. At one point Mary recalls saying to her mom, "I'm jealous. I want to be part of this party. It was like a big party." Then, "in the middle of it all, she was talking to someone. I tried to talk to them too, and she turned and looked at me and she said, 'No, not you. This is my world, and this is where I'm going. You got to stay here and stay in that world.'" At other points "she would say things like 'I can't do this.' Or 'This is so hard.'"

The final night, Mary's mother slid off the bed two times. "I'm like, 'You cannot be sliding off the bed because if we're going to do this, I have to have a back, a working back.'" Mary got her mom back into bed, "and that's when she saw the angel. She's talking to all these people and blah, blah, blah, and it was just normal, and then she was pointing and reaching and gasping. I said, 'What is it?' and she said, 'It's an angel,' and I said, 'Really? What does it look like?' and she said, 'Oh, she's so beautiful,' and, of course, at that point I was like, 'Oh my God, we're not in Kansas anymore.'

"I'm trying to feel the angel. I'm trying to see and feel the angel, but it's just all so much for me to take in, and I am overwhelmed. I'm trying to make sure she's okay, but my whole body was just tingling and feeling like I'm in the presence of God.

"It was like Godness, and it was like the room became a different room. The room became bigger than it is, softer than it is, and not of this world anymore. We were not on the earth plane. I was here, but part of me was in it with her and I was just completely taken over by it. It was like they were showing me that there's something else, and you don't have to worry. There's something else, God or whatever it is, and I don't have to worry about what to do.

"It was as if they're coming to get her, there's a force so big that it would be able to pierce the worlds and come and get her, and I don't have to worry about her or anything. That was the message for me."

Reflecting now, Mary says, "When I first started taking care of her here, I was just following my inner guidance. There was no one else to do it. The whole two years, I didn't know that this was going to be the gift at the end. That I would be shown that there is something so powerful." Although her family was Catholic, Mary says, "I'm not a religious person. I'm more like a blend of pagan and Buddhist, but the godliness that was there was so obvious, and then all the beings were inside that godliness. It was like if my ancestors were a band, then God was the backer behind it. God was the producer, and they were all there."

She adds, "I did feel a big well of grief after, but the grief is now walking next to the godliness." The comfort, she notes, has been "to know that there's a plan, there's some kind of a divine orchestration to life, and that's really the message I felt was coming through. I felt like a gift. It was mostly about her, but somehow I was lucky enough to be there."

One of the most detailed descriptions of "beautiful, noble beings of light" that I have encountered comes from Celia B., who helped care for her mother, but was not present at her bedside when she passed. In many ways, her story captures the breadth, the power, and ultimately the healing possibilities of the shared death experience.

"My mom was about as energetic, athletic, and active a woman as you can imagine, but then she was diagnosed with non-Hodgkin's lymphoma. They treated it with chemo and radiation, but one of the side effects was that her nerve sheaths were destroyed, and she lost the ability to walk. For her to be bound to a wheelchair and in horrible pain was very hard. It got to the point where Dad couldn't care for her. She moved to assisted living, where she was bedridden. She had aides come in to care for her. They had to use a crane to get her out of bed.

"In her retirement community, the residents were reading a book by a Harvard physician about dying with dignity. He was essentially saying that our modern medical system is so geared to keeping people alive, regardless of their quality of life, that we've really lost something here. It became all the talk of the seniors in this community. After several months in assisted living, my mom made the courageous decision to end her own life by stopping eating and drinking. She didn't feel like she was living with dignity. With the pain meds, she often felt out of it. She felt her quality of life was gone.

"Soon in her little retirement community, the word got out about Marie: Marie's going to end her life. But the administration couldn't allow this. They would lose their license in Massachusetts, so we had to move Mom back into the town house with Dad. We got a hospital bed for her in the living room, and we set up hospice. We learned that the process takes about two weeks.

"Prior to this, the burden of caring for Mom had been on my dad and sister. I would fly back from California and stay for a couple of weeks at a time to give them both a break. When Mom made this decision, I made the choice to go be with her for the full two weeks, with my father, brother, and sister assisting. I offered to be in charge of the meds and to help make sure that the aides and hospice workers were giving her the right meds for pain. That was a hard role for a daughter to be in because Mom would sometimes emerge from her stupor and be in a lot of pain and be angry and calling, 'Where are my meds?' And she knew that I was in charge of them. I'd have to call hospice or the doctor, and many times I would have to tell her that I had given her all she was allowed.

"We did have two wonderful family evenings where she was in fine form. We ordered Chinese one night, and my father, sister, brother, and I were all there. Mom cracked us up. She had control over her hospital bed, and she pushed the button. It started to lift up and she said, 'I am rising from my sarcophagus.' Then my brother joked, 'You are our mummy, after all.' We all had a good laugh about this. Then we told stories, shared memories, and sang songs.

"In the second week, she was sleeping a lot more. On Saturday, two days before she died, I was so wrung out, I told my father that I needed to go spend the night in a hotel. We had gone for a hike to get out, and when we returned, she wasn't speaking anymore. I still feel so sad about this. Mom was really out of it on Sunday. My brother played fiddle for her.

"I spent another night in the hotel; my brother went home to Maine, and my sister was home at her own house. I woke early in the morning, and I began my meditation practice, as I always try to do. As I was meditating, I felt really guided to meditate on the clear light. I didn't know what it was at the time; I just trusted it. I remember resting in this clear, beautiful spaciousness. Then I had an image of my mom, not her features so much, but I could tell it was her energy. She was surrounded by these beautiful, noble beings of light. They were tall, taller than her, and they surrounded her. They didn't have any descriptive features, but they were beautiful in their demeanor. There were maybe six or eight of them. It was so beautiful, the energy of it, and the way they were holding her. There was such a sense of everything's going to be okay. I remember I sat there and watched this, and it really was a message for me that all will be well. Your mom is okay.

"I sat with that image for a while and then it passed. And I remember thinking, 'Well, that was interesting.' A little past eight, I called my dad to plan for the day, and he said, 'Your mom just died.' I raced over, and she was gone from her body. I remember embracing my dad, who was crying. And I said prayers and blessings over her body, and we put a beautiful flower on her chest. And then the funeral home came and wrapped her up and took her off.

"And as they were carrying her off, my dad was distraught, and I hugged him, and I told him what I had seen, and he started to cry again. He's not a religious or spiritual man, but I think to hear what my experience had been was comforting for him, and I had also been able to tell him how Mom loves you so much and you'll never be apart. The words came through me, but it was clearly a message for him.

"A few days later, we went over to one of his neighbors' for cocktails outside, there were probably five of his friends, all in their eighties. And Dad said, 'Celia, tell them about your experience.' It was really, I thought, remarkable that he got it, and it resonated with him. He's someone who, if I went on a meditation, would ask me, 'How was your séance?' I was just thrilled that my experience could act as a message that was comforting to Dad and to his friends."

In the time that has passed since her experience, Celia has reflected on that early morning, and says she wonders "if by meditating on the clear light, maybe I was supporting Mom or helping
Mom, or something like that."

The experience of seeing and knowing that there were visible
guides or angelic beings appearing around the time of death to care
for and assist their loved ones has been transformative for Stephanie, Mary, and Celia. Additionally, in presenting the events, each
woman refers in various forms to the concept of a "gift" to describe
this experience. The concept that shared death experiencers have
received a special gift and been granted special insight embedded
in the loss of their loved one is among the most universal themes
expressed by the wide range of individuals whose cases we have
reviewed.

However, the cases of Stephanie, Mary, and Celia also speak
to another phenomenon that we have found as we compile these
shared-death-experience accounts: of the individuals reporting
SDEs, 85 percent are women. We can theorize that this is due in
part to the traditional role of women as caregivers and perhaps to
women being more engaged in some spiritual practice. But overwhelmingly, the SDE message seems to be received more openly by
women. The reason for this continues to perplex and fascinate me,
not simply as a researcher, but as a therapist and a man who works
almost exclusively with families and individuals coping with the end
of life.

7

TRAUMA AND SDEs

UP TO now, we have largely explored events in which death, even when sudden, was not entirely unexpected. There was declining health, serious illness, premature birth, or a terrible accident that had left its victim in a coma. Even the language we use to discuss these moments captures their fragility: we talk about "fighting for life" or "clinging to life." We recognize that vitality and longevity are not certainties. But there are other forms of death for which nearly all of us are completely unprepared. Among those, trauma, overdose, and suicide are three of the most devastating. Every year, more than 150,000 people in the United States die from injury, often sudden trauma, and many of these people are young, just entering the prime of their lives. Drug overdoses annually claim upward of 50,000 victims—in 2020, during the Covid pandemic, the number of US overdose deaths skyrocketed to more

than 90,000. Roughly two-thirds of the more than 900,000 overdoses that have occurred in the last two decades have involved some
form of opiates. The number of deaths from suicide often closely
matches the number of overdoses; almost 50,000 lives are lost in
this manner each year. One question that galvanized me as I began
this work and exploration was whether it was possible to have a
shared death experience around such a sudden and shattering event,
and, if so, how would trauma impact the way an SDE was experienced? I wondered: Is there even a time or an opportunity for communication to occur? Or would the trauma somehow block an SDE
from occurring? And if an SDE did occur, what would that mean for
the dying and those left behind? The short answer is that SDEs are
possible, and they take different forms. Four individuals who have
experienced traumatic loss shared their stories with me, about both
the event and what they have personally come to understand about
both sudden death and their own SDE in its aftermath.

Traumatic losses can be among the hardest for any of us to comprehend. How many of us would struggle to find the words to try
to extend comfort to a family in which there has been a suicide, or
overdose, or a horrific accident? Indeed, in the face of tragedy, I have
counseled many bereaved family and friends who have faced the
second devastation of having longtime personal supports turn away
when the manner of death is revealed. In this context, it takes significant courage to talk about SDEs and to discuss what happened.

When we first spoke to Dawn B., it was clear that she had
courage. "I feel like I'm a good coper. I can handle a lot of things;
the more you throw at me, the better I am. I've been working in
the emergency room for eighteen years, and so I see death quite

frequently. I take care of death. When I was about thirty, and returning to school for my registered nursing degree, I also worked for a tissue banking company, which harvests skin, bones, stuff like that. I did that for two years. I've always been respectful of spirits and souls and those type of things.

"I have three children. Sean was twenty-eight at the time. Shane was twenty-five, and my daughter was twenty-four. Sean was born when I was eighteen. I married my high school sweetheart. We got divorced, and I remarried.

"Sean went into the navy. After he got out, he traveled, and he went to work at Sears. He had the highest sales every month. He lived paycheck to paycheck, but he never complained. Once a week we'd have lunch by Sears. He had this wonderfully dry humor and kind of James Dean hair. He was going back to school to study computers. We took a college contemporary literature class together, and we used to discuss the books. He was just a chill kid.

"It was May 15, 2017, the day after Mother's Day, and Sean was five days away from getting married. It was about eleven o'clock in the morning, and Sean gave me a call. I met him for lunch, with one of his friends, and my daughter. We enjoyed each other, laughed, talked." Sean was waiting for his paycheck on Friday, so Dawn went to her car to give him some extra cash. His bachelor party was that night. "I was gonna give him cash, but I had forgotten that I had given my cash to my mom for Mother's Day. And he patted me on the shoulder, and he said, 'No worries.' A couple of hours later, he sent me a text and it said, 'You're the best.' And I said, 'Why do you say that?' He said, 'Because you are.' I had already transferred a hundred dollars to his bank account, and I told him, 'I don't want your friends paying for everything. I'd like for you to pay for something.'"

Sean and his friends "went out to a little place where they adver-
tised Ping-Pong. There were six of them, and the whole group was
playing Ping-Pong. Sean broke a Ping-Pong paddle, and he and his bud-
dies walked across the street to the Walmart to purchase a new one,
but it wasn't a regular Walmart, it was a grocery Walmart. So they
went to CVS, and purchased some snacks and some beer. They were
crossing back across the road, and a car hit two of them in the group.

"I was home, hot-gluing flowers on this big selfie board for the
wedding. I was texting Sean's fiancée, Tessa, saying, 'Do you like this?
Do you know what this is?' And she said, 'Is that tissue paper?' And
I was writing her back saying, 'Yes.' And I was writing, 'Y-E-S. And I
got the Y out, and then suddenly, I couldn't see the phone. I couldn't
see anything. My feet came off the floor. I felt like I was gonna pass
out, and I got real nauseated. I scooted this bench up under me, and
I looked behind me because we had all these flowers on the kitchen
floor through the hallway, and real strong, all of a sudden, I felt,
SEAN IS DEAD. In my mind, I said, 'We're wasting our time. Sean
won't be able to enjoy these flowers.'

"At 10:31, I got a call from Tessa to tell me that Sean had been
hit by a car, and I said to myself, 'This happened at 10:27.' Nearly
five minutes before. A week or so later, we're in the DMV and we're
taking Sean's vehicles and transferring them into our names, and
the accident report says, 'Time of injury: 22:28.' That's the time
of the 911 call. I said, 'See, I told you guys this happened at 10:27,
a minute before the 911 call, because I told my family, my friends,
everybody, that something happened to me. I can't explain it. But I
told everyone, from Catholics to Baptists to people who don't believe in anything, 'I felt it. I felt what happened. I felt the accident. I
could tell you exactly the moment.'

"My husband, Toby, drove me to the hospital. And I told him when we got into the car that Sean was dead. He's a trauma nurse, and he will tell you, you can never rely solely on what somebody tells you over the phone. He kept saying, 'You need to wait until we get there and realize what happened, just to see what his condition is.' But I kept telling him over and over that Sean was gone. I already knew. They took him to the hospital where Toby works, and when we arrived, Toby went in and listened to the EMS report. I stood out in the ambulance bay. We got there before the ambulance. He came out and said, 'It's bad, they're gonna intubate him when he gets here.' And I said, 'Okay.'" When Sean came off the ambulance, he was already intubated.

"I remember the neurologist's blue gloves. He came in and told us that he couldn't save him, it was the type of brain injury that you can't save. Sean lived for fourteen more hours, his body did. I told his fiancée, 'Put down the bedrail and get in bed with him. Spend time with his soul.' But when I said it, I knew his soul wasn't in that body anymore.

"I had hundreds of people coming to my house because we were getting ready for a wedding. Now we were going to bury Sean the day before his wedding. I had air mattresses in my living room, and I literally tiptoed over people to get to the computer, and all I could research was, 'Can a soul go through your body? What happens when a soul leaves the body? Can a soul leave prior to death?'

"In the beginning, I used to say, 'Do you believe me?' And I used to tell everybody, 'This is what happened.' Now I don't care who believes me and who doesn't believe me. I'm not looking for proof. I know one hundred percent in my soul what happened to me."

When Dawn was forty, she was diagnosed with triple negative

breast cancer. She recalls sitting on the back porch of her house with Sean, both of them crying, and him asking her, "Mom, how did you get this?" She told him that she was raised in the 1970s, when McDonald's and Coca-Cola "were the thing." Sean would encourage her by saying, "You're the strongest woman I know." She adds, "And I thought about that so many times, especially right after. I'd think, 'Did he come to me to let me know, for me to be strong?'"

Dawn is a can-do, unfussy person, with a practical, straight haircut and glasses. She avoids makeup, and it's clear from a glance around her walls that she adores her grandchildren. But it is impossible to miss the conviction in her voice when she discusses the aftermath of her experience. "I've gone through normal grieving and normal coping, but I think it's been better because of my experience. I believe in a God. I do believe that I'll see Sean again one day, spiritually. I'm not afraid of death, I never have been, but I think I'm just more comfortable if God should take me today."

Most of all, Dawn says, "I will stand on my rooftop as a normal, average American who makes average money, who has an average life, who has three decent children and doesn't take any medicine, and say, 'This is what happened to me. I felt my son as he passed from this earth.'"

Another powerful example of the shared death experience around sudden death involves the very specific trauma of a drug overdose. Consider the stories of Sarah M. and Jackie P., two among more than a million left behind by the toll of the current epidemic.

Sarah spent twenty-seven years as a firefighter in California. The youngest of five children, she grew up in a military family, moving around from post to post. She describes herself as a "spiritually inclusive Christian." She has also studied Buddhism; one sister converted to Judaism. Sarah notes that she is close to all her nieces and nephews—"I love them all"—but particularly close to her oldest sister's two daughters. "They went to high school near me, they have been in my life." Sarah would text her niece Leila throughout the week. After graduating from college, Leila became a journalist and traveled the world. She married and gave birth to her own daughter, and then divorced. Sarah recalls that Leila was "very bright, but she was troubled. I think we missed it. As a firefighter, I saw lots of drugs and alcohol. My sister's a nurse, but somehow we missed it with Leila."

Leila settled in Boston, but she continued drinking. Sarah's sister had traveled east and spent six weeks trying to get her "stable." Leila was having a difficult time with being a single mom and with her job. It was November 2016. Sarah recalls, "I was texting with Leila, and I said, 'How are you doing without your mom?' She said, 'Great, but now it's time for some Leila time.'" A day passed. Then at 3:45 on Sunday morning, Sarah recalls that she "woke up abruptly with a severe cramp in my leg. I've had cramps before, but nothing like this." Sarah leaped out of bed and began jumping up and down, waking her husband. What came next was terrifying: "This part, I don't remember. I was stiff and seizing. My eyes were rolling back in my head." Both of their college-age kids were home and Sarah's husband yelled for them to call 911. Sarah came to, said she was okay, and her daughter canceled the ambulance. "I looked at my son, and I said, 'That was the strangest experience. This is what it feels like to die.'" Next, Sarah began to sweat profusely. "I drenched the sheets for about two hours, and then vomited. I called my sister and she said I should go to the doctor. But I felt normal, other than being a little wiped out. I canceled my choir commitment, and then twenty minutes later, my sister called back to say that Leila had died." She had snorted fentanyl-laced heroin.

Almost immediately Sarah felt that her niece had been reaching out, particularly "because of my feeling that this is what it feels like to die. I began processing that maybe I had a visit from Leila on some level, on a spiritual level."

To the question of what do you think happens after we die, Sarah responds, "I think about that a lot. I think there's a transformation that we may not understand. I don't think we are walking around above the clouds in the same physical bodies in a heavenly state, but I think there's definitely another plane, and we'll go to that plane. I think we'll have consciousness.

"I'm intrigued," she adds. "I don't want to go there yet, but I'm not afraid."

Jackie is in her forties and works with special needs students in the province of British Columbia, Canada. "I was having a regular night," she recalls. "About one or two a.m., I felt this sharp, horrible pain in my chest. I was feeling it all in my arms. They were tingling. It was really horrible, and I didn't know what was going on. I phoned my girlfriend and I told her I didn't know if I was having a heart attack or a panic attack. I said, 'I'm terrified, so please just stay on the phone with me, and if something happens, phone the ambulance.' She was trying to calm me down, and I felt like the room was spinning. I felt a serious sense of doom, like something bad was happening."

In the midst of this, Jackie began to see the eyes of the man whom she considered her lifelong best friend—"Luke would come to my house almost daily, I'd feed him dinner. I loved him, but he was kind of a womanizer. My dad was a big womanizer, and I didn't want to follow in my mother's footsteps, so I told him I loved him, but I couldn't be with him."

Now, in this moment in the middle of the night, Jackie saw his blue eyes. She remembers they were "kind of glossy and dead. I didn't know what this was about," she adds. "I thought I was dying, so I was like, 'What does this have to do with him?'" The episode passed, but "the image of Luke's dead eyes kept coming into my head. It was almost like I was seeing him." At 8 a.m., she received a call that Luke had died. "The worst part was, I wasn't surprised. Most people would be in denial that their best friend died, and I felt so horrible because part of me knew that he died." When she pieced the story together, she realized that "the time that I thought I was having a heart attack was approximately the time that he OD'd on fentanyl."

Jackie went to a doctor within a couple of days. "He said I'm healthier than healthy and nothing's wrong with my heart." Jackie began to consider other possibilities, explaining, "My friend Catherine, who was on the phone with me, put the pieces together and said, 'What if you shared in his death?'"

A few months later, while Jackie was riding her bike, a car suddenly entered the bike path. "At the last minute I turned my wheel, something forced me to turn my wheel, I heard a voice that said, 'Turn your wheel.' I was able to go over the hood of the car instead of under the car. I got away with a lot of broken bones, but I was alive. It's just a really strange coincidence that in the same year Luke dies, I got to live. I should have been, honestly, dead. The paramedic told me that I was seriously lucky to be alive." Jackie also notes that she is mother to an autistic son. "My son cannot live without me, and I know Luke would have done anything for me and my son." Again, Catherine said to Jackie, "I bet he saved your life because he loved you and your son so much!"

Jackie began searching for information online, which eventually led her to the Shared Crossing Project. Her experience has also led her to reevaluate her thoughts around death. "I skipped a few stages of the grief. I definitely didn't have denial. I knew Luke was dead.

"I'm kind of terrified of death now, because I honestly felt that he suffered and was terrified; what he was feeling, I was feeling. He was scared." But she adds, "I used to think this was a really negative thing, but Catherine put it in a different perspective, that he cared about you so much and now you know how much he cares about you because he wanted to share this with you." Ultimately, Jackie says that this experience led her to figure out that "I did love Luke, and I believe he loved me too.

"It's just so hard because he was so vibrant when he was alive. He loved life so much, and it's so hard to have somebody who loved life get taken by a stupid drug. He was a social user. He got a bad batch because now they stick fentanyl in everything. He did it, and he died."

Jackie's own search for answers continues. "I used to be an atheist," she told us. "Now, I don't know. I really don't know."

While both Sarah and Jackie had their shared death experiences at night in their homes, we have also found that the experiencer may be touched in an unexpected time and location. That's the case for longtime friends Richard K. and Pat. The two met in Harrisburg, Pennsylvania, through their volunteer work with the Contact Helpline, a twenty-four-hour regional helpline for people in need of local services. Some callers wanted to vent, and some were in need of help or direction.

Richard came to Contact after working with the Pennsylvania Department of Education and with a background in educational testing. He had a doctorate in educational psychology. Pat worked as the office manager for a group of neurologists and was the divorced mother of two teenagers, but volunteering at Contact appealed to her. "She was very empathetic," Richard recalls. "She was a superb listener. It seemed like she hardly needed to be trained, she was just that good."

Richard and Pat were often matched to provide training and workshop presentations and were not shy about kidding each other over the smallest of details. "Contact asked us all to take personality tests, such as the Myers-Briggs Type Indicator, and my type profile was introvert, intuitive, thinking, and judging—INTJ. Pat would tease me and say, 'Well, your J must be slipping. You are becoming more flexible all the time.'" But Richard was also one of the first people she told when she began wrestling with the decision to change her career path and become an ordained Methodist minister. She spoke to him of hearing a calling to "feed my sheep."

"Pat had been raised Catholic," he adds. "In fact, she gave birth to her first child in a Catholic hospital. She was twenty-four, but she looked about sixteen years old. One of the nuns helping in the hospital was not very congenial toward Pat up until she was discharged. Then the nun looked at Pat's chart and apologized. She had assumed that Pat was an unwed teenage mother rather than a young married woman. I've always remembered that story because at the same age, I was also embarrassed about looking much younger."

Pat initially told Richard that she felt unworthy, but she did eventually enroll in a seminary, married another Methodist pastor, and helped organize the Center for Spiritual Formation, a place that serves as a resource for people seeking a deeper relationship with God. Pat also codeveloped the center's two-year program, known as the Ministry of Spiritual Direction, designed to provide enhanced training for church pastors and laypeople. "She was just such an approachable person. She put everyone at ease," Richard recalls.

A dementia diagnosis in her early seventies forced Pat to retire from the profession she loved. "I remember a conversation we had after her diagnosis," Richard says. "She told me that the doctors had been recommending certain medications that might possibly slow the process but would not stop it. Having worked in a medical practice, she was familiar with many of them, and the others she had looked up. When she studied the side effects, she told me she thought, 'I don't know which is worse, the disease or the medications meant to relieve its symptoms.'"

About six months before her death, Pat told Richard, "I'm losing the capacity to know who it is I'm talking to or seeing." Her husband, Dennis, shared that several times Pat had been unable to recognize her daughter or her grandchildren. Dennis said that she had told him, "I should know those people."

Reflecting on that period, Richard, now in his early eighties, says, "I'm thinking this was part of what led to her death, because her death was by suicide. She had awoken before Dennis and had gone to the kitchen area, where there were various medications on the counter. She basically knew enough to recognize that if she took the entire contents of these different medications in combination, it would end her life. I personally think she did not want to be a burden on anyone. I think it was, knowing her, an act of courage on her part to relieve other people of that burden, and probable financial burden as well.

"Dennis called me to say that Pat had been taken to the emergency room and that things did not look good." He called again the next morning to tell Richard that Pat had died. "I was just numb," Richard recalls. "Other than my wife, Pat was my best friend.

"In the afternoon, I decided I needed to get outside and walk. Physically, I was just walking automatically. I couldn't really think. I was numb with grief as well."

Then Richard began to have an all-consuming experience. It started with visual phenomena. "I had this strange sensation, a sense of something in front of me and slightly above my head almost. It was something sparkly, and that caught me by surprise. The next thing I was aware of was that I had a strong sense of Pat's presence."

Richard describes seeing an image of Pat: "I could see her dancing, dancing for joy. The words that came to me were *free at last, free of her pain*." Richard immediately found himself "caught up in her expression of joy." That joy was so powerful and pervasive that it lifted his own numbness and grief. Rather than "just trudging along, I'm energized. Her joy was my joy."

After this SDE, Richard periodically experienced Pat's presence in dreams. The final one occurred in June 2019. He woke with emotions that were so strong that he felt Pat must be saying goodbye. Richard describes "feeling an intense love that I imagined her being bathed in, an intense, all-encompassing love that pervades the universe. For a brief period of time, I was probably experiencing what she was experiencing. From that, I take enormous comfort. I have tremendous gratitude, unspeakable gratitude.

"Even though there are times when I will think of Pat and how much I miss her, that sense of joy is still there. It never left. That's incredible healing in a fraction of a second, enormous comfort."

In many ways, Richard's experience parallels Alison A.'s vision of her good friend Wendy, not only in terms of what they saw but also in terms of the emotions conveyed to them in that moment, particularly joy, freedom, and release. Significantly as well, both Wendy and Pat had faced serious health challenges. Richard did ultimately share his story with Dennis, Pat's husband. "I'm sure he had great disappointment that he himself didn't have an experience like that. But it was also reassuring to him. He got comfort from Pat having made that transition to another state of consciousness."

Frequently, one of the most powerful parts of the SDE for the experiencers is how they use what they participated in to reframe and reassess their own emotions and processes of grief. That is particularly true for SDEs that occur around trauma or sudden passing, because of the challenging range of emotions associated with those losses. As a counselor, I have found that the experiencers' personal pathways to reach their own interpretation and understanding of what has transpired between themselves and the person they cared about are deeply powerful, deeply meaningful, and deeply healing, even for a traumatic loss. I sit in awe and appreciation of what they are able to share.

8

THE SDE IN
MULTIPLE FORMS

LOSS, AS we have come to understand, is a central fact of life. And most of us will experience the passing of multiple loved ones and friends during our lifetimes. Within that space, some individuals will also be the recipients of multiple shared death experiences. We have already glimpsed this process earlier in the book with Michelle, who had an SDE with both of her children, and Madelyn, who had SDEs with her mother and her friend Chayim. Now let us explore this process directly with three individuals who connected with loved ones in various aspects of death. Significantly, they participated in different ways with each passing, and they also experienced different sensations connected to each event. One of their SDEs may be synchronous with the time of death, another could be asynchronous. These cases also highlight the fact that while some SDEs have very strong phenomenological components, with bright light and greeting parties and many elements, other SDEs occur with a different type of connection. And the connection need not be grand to be deeply meaningful. Those individual nuances explicitly highlight the complexity and individuality of each SDE.

Lula C. grew up in two churches, Baptist and Pentecostal. "My mom and dad were both just wonderful Christians, really loved the Lord, and taught us well." The hardest differences for Lula between the two faiths were the requirements around dressing. "In my mom's faith, Pentecostal, we couldn't wear makeup, we couldn't wear short-sleeved blouses, we couldn't wear shoes with the toes out." Women could only wear "powder on their face, but no lipstick, no eyeliner, no blush. I had some difficulties with that, but what would happen is that on Halloween, I would always want to dress up, wear makeup. I would dress up, put my makeup on. The next morning, I didn't wash my face because I wanted to wear it to school. But other than that, as far as the teaching, the two faiths were very, very similar. Our family really enjoyed being in both faiths and learned a lot from both."

Lula was one of eight children. Her dad worked in a steel mill, but her parents moved from Alabama to Detroit when she was three years old to give their children opportunities outside of the segregated South. She recalls her mom as the person in the family whom others sought out to help explain or interpret their dreams. "They would ask her, 'Hattie, what does this mean?' So, I do believe I acquired what I am getting from my different experiences from my mom."

As an adult, Lula's primary spiritual connection was first through the Baptist Church, and then, after she divorced and remarried, she joined a nondenominational church with her second husband. "My new husband—well, not new, we've been married almost forty-some years, but he's Lutheran, so we tend to go to a nondenominational church, which is satisfying for both of us."

Lula maintained a busy work life, finding employment at a tire company for seventeen years, then starting a janitorial service in California. When her second husband, Luther, was given the opportunity to run a company in San Antonio, Texas, she sold her business to follow him and went to work for a large insurance company. She also spent time volunteering in the community, including taking her sons to visit elderly nursing home residents. "I'm the type of person who likes to give something back to the community. So I would go to the nursing homes, speak to the patients, say, 'Hi, how are you today? Hello. How are you?' And they knew me up there. I would take my kids so we can just say hello to the patients. One of the directors gave me her card."

Both Lula's and Luther's families remained in Detroit. Lula explains: "My mother-in-law lived in Detroit. As she was getting older, I would fly back and forth when her health failed. She was also caring for my husband's brother, Larry, who suffered from paranoid schizophrenia. It came to a point, I just told my husband, 'We just can't leave her there by herself any longer.' But she said no. I went to Detroit. I called my sisters and a couple of my friends. I said, 'I need some prayers. I'm here in Detroit. I would like you to pray for me that we'll be able to get my mother-in-law to Texas.' She kept saying no. She didn't want to live with us, she said, 'What's going to happen with Larry?' And I said, 'Larry can come too.' I told her we would take Larry, and she finally agreed to move.

"I called Luther. I said, 'Luther, your mom has agreed to come.'

He said, 'Lula, how did you do that?' I said, 'I didn't do it. I prayed over it and the Lord answered my prayers. But she doesn't want to stay with us.' He said, 'Well, what is she going to do?' I said, 'Luther, in my closet there's a card for the director at the nursing home where the kids and I have been going. Call her, tell her who you are and why you're calling.' The nursing facility had one bed available. So Luther says, 'Lula, they have a bed for Mom.'

"The night of her death, I went up to the nursing home to see her and said, 'Hi, Mom, how are you?' For two days, she didn't want to eat. Before that, whenever I would leave, she would say to me, 'So long!' She never, ever, ever said goodbye to me, she said, 'So long!'

"That night I was trying to encourage her to eat. She would take maybe just a little spoonful of Jell-O, and we talked until I left. I said, 'Okay, Mom, I'm going to go now. I'll see you tomorrow.' And when I got to the door, she said, 'Goodbye.' I didn't respond, I just ran out of there, because she'd never, ever, ever said goodbye to me. I got in my car, and I sat there, and I just prayed to the Lord, and I cried, I just cried. Because that goodbye to me meant we were going to lose her. I got myself together; I drove back home.

"Luther was upstairs in the office. I told him, 'I went to see your mom. Luther, when I left, she said goodbye to me.' And I started crying. He said, 'Lula, just relax, just rest.' And I told him, 'But she's never said goodbye to me, Luther.' I go downstairs, and about fifteen minutes later, I start coughing. I mean, an uncontrollable cough. I coughed and I coughed. Luther said, 'What's wrong with you?' I said, 'I don't know. I just can't quit coughing.' He said, 'Lula, Lula, get some water, get some water.' I kept coughing and coughing. And then I stopped. About ten or fifteen minutes later, the phone rang, and that was the nursing home calling Luther to make him aware that my mother-in-law had passed.

"I thought about that later, and then I thought, 'Wow. What was she trying to say? What was she doing? Why did I cough?' I wondered if she was having difficulty breathing. But I think I was there with her. I just felt a closeness. I've often thought, 'Why was I there?' I think she wanted me to be there.

"After she passed, there were times I could hear her or sense her saying, 'Take care of Larry.' And I would say, 'Yes, we are definitely going to take care of Larry. We're going to take care of Larry, Mom.' That was the main focus that I felt from her after she passed, that we would definitely take care of her son, and we did take care of him for twenty-one years."

Lula's experience of shared physical sensations partially parallels Sarah's and Jackie's experiences from the previous chapter, but it contains another key component: a predeath premonition. Becoming aware of an impending death can be a facet of an SDE. Sometimes these predeath realizations occur close to the death; other times, they may take place at a greater distance in time from the actual event. Lula would have a second such predeath experience, similar to what she'd had surrounding the loss of her mother-in-law.

"My daughter, Felicia, had been diagnosed with sarcoidosis [a disease that attacks the lungs]. She was in denial for a couple of years, and she got pregnant with a baby boy, against the doctors' suggestions. Randal was born two months premature in March. In November, Felicia called me and said, 'Hi, Mom!' and told me, 'Well, you're going to be a grandmother again.' I could not say congratulations, because her delivery of Randal had been so difficult. I'm thinking, *Oh gosh, Felicia*. She said, 'Mom, I'm okay. Just pray for me. Mom, you know you pray a lot, and I also pray a lot. Mom, I'm going to be fine.' "

Lula had recently completed a training class for hospice volunteers when her own mother's health began to deteriorate. She flew to Detroit to spend the remaining time with her mother and was with her when she died. Lula recalls, "I called Felicia, and she's four and a half months pregnant. I say, 'Grandma passed away.' I didn't say, 'Don't come to the funeral.' But I just assumed that with her being pregnant and working, she's probably not going to come. We are at the funeral and my sister says, 'Lu, it sounds like someone's in the back on a breathing machine.' And I turned around, and there was Felicia, walking down the aisle with baby Randal.

"I told her to get some rest, but she flew home to California the next day. A few weeks later, in May, I had a dream, but it was so real. I will tell it like it's a real story, this is how real it was. Felicia was visiting us in Texas, and I got up out of bed to take her to the airport. I drop her off, and she goes in. And when I came back home, I walk into my brother-in-law Larry's room, which was right by the garage. I came in through the garage, and I looked in his room. I said, 'Larry, what's the bundle in your bed?' He said, 'I don't know.' So I go over to the bundle, I pull back the comforter, and there was baby Randal. I started saying, 'Oh my gosh! Felicia left Randal! Oh my gosh, Felicia left Randal!' And then I woke up.

"Luther said to me, 'Lula, Lula, Lula, you're having a dream.' I told him about this dream. I said, 'Luther. Felicia left Randal. He was just as real as I'm looking at you.' He said, 'Lula, it was a dream.' I said, 'Luther, you don't understand. Felicia left Randal.' Luther said, 'Lula, just relax. It was a dream.' I got up, and I go to work that day, and on my break, instead of going to the break room, I just walked around in the parking lot just praying to the Lord, just praying to the Lord.

"I called my son-in-law, and he said, 'Oh, Mom, Felicia had the worst night last night. I thought I was going to lose her.' So I don't tell him about the dream because I don't want to frighten him. I talked to Felicia, and she said, 'Mom, just pray for me, just pray for me. Mom, I'll be fine.' Two weeks later, on Memorial Day, I got the call that 'Felicia's fighting for her life.' We lost Felicia and her unborn baby."

But that was not Lula's final connection with Felicia. Not long after her daughter's funeral, Lula had an experience that has stayed with her for two decades. "Luther's out of the country on a business trip, and I'm asleep. I had just started using a CPAP machine because my breathing was stopping during the night. But the mask didn't fit me well, and I was taking it off. As I was sleeping, I felt someone touch my side twice. I woke up and realized I had snatched the mask off, and I had almost certainly stopped breathing. My first thought was that Felicia was there. I sat on the side of the bed, and I could still feel her touch. In my heart, I know that Felicia woke me up. That was Felicia saying, 'Mom, wake up.' She didn't want anything to happen to me. She wanted me to be there for Randal."

Lula's grandson, whose mom died when he was fifteen months old, is now in college. She has been there for him for more than twenty years.

We have discussed the appearance of energy and the sensation of heightened energy around the SDE for the experiencer. In some ways, Lula's sensations—the coughing she experienced with her mother-in-law's passing and the feeling of her daughter's touch, waking her up not long after the funeral—can be seen as forms of energetic connection. These moments are also reminders that an SDE need not have many grand features to be profoundly meaningful and life changing to the experiencer. Finally, Lula's experience contains another element that we touched upon briefly in the case of Adela B., and will encounter again in several other cases: post-death visitation. How connected do we remain, and in what form, to our loved ones after they have passed?

For our next case, we encounter both a post-death visitation and physical sensations on an entirely different continent and in a different context: Javier was born in Spain and raised in a religious, Catholic family, although he adds that, from a recent DNA test, he discovered that he has a lot of Jewish background on his father's side. Most likely what happened, he believes, was that part of his family converted to Catholicism during the Spanish Inquisition. "I am a translator," he explains. "I have studied languages and linguistics. At the moment I work as a narrator for TV commercials in Spain and a voice actor as well. I was featured in several films too."

His first experience occurred after the death of his younger brother. While it is not a traditional SDE and, as an experience, it falls more into the category of a post-death visitation, for Javier, it did have a similar impact to an SDE. "My brother died in 1989 at age twenty-seven. I was very attached to him because I was one year older. For several years, I was thinking a lot about him, and I was missing him a lot, and I was very sad about that.

"I am gay, and I was living in London in an apartment with my boyfriend at the time, Paul. We're still in touch, and we always comment on that episode. The spirit of my brother came into the building, and we started to communicate. I was not fast asleep; I was semiconscious, and I was hugging my brother. We were talking, and he was communicating. He basically told me that he was okay, that I shouldn't be worried about him. I was crying, crying in my dream without tears, but really feeling like I was crying, and told him that I loved him very, very much. He said, 'Now I need to leave.' I said, 'Don't.' He said, 'Yes, I need to leave.' He said goodbye. He left."

After Javier's brother's spirit departed, Paul awoke. He was disoriented, but he was acutely aware that there had been another presence in the room. Javier recalls, "Paul said to me, 'Yes, I could feel it. I could feel something strange that I was not by myself.'" Time has not diminished the strength of the experience, either for Javier or Paul. "It's just reality," Javier observes. "We both believe it, even Paul, who is very skeptical. It's one of those things that happened. My brother came to let me know that he was fine, just to bring peace to me."

Javier rarely spoke of what happened with his mother, even though he says, "The thing is, my mother, we had a very good relationship. She was very spiritual. We were able to discuss a lot of things about death and about life after death. One time, in the hospital, she had a near-death experience. I'm very skeptical. I used to tell her, 'When we die, we go to the memorable place we come from.' Or I would say that we were going to a place that was 'very hot.' I was telling her just to tease her a little bit. I never told her about my brother coming to me because I never discussed with my mother my sexuality or things like that, but we used to talk a lot about life, and we had a good connection. We were six brothers.

I have five brothers and one sister. With me, she had this connection where she would talk about more spiritual things than she did with the rest of her sons.

"The last three months of her life, my mother was doing very poorly. I went to see her in January, and she passed away the sixth of March. I had talked to my sister and she said, 'Mom is weak and feeble, but she's okay.' I was not expecting my mother to die that day.

"I was sleeping, and about five o'clock in the morning, I noticed that I was sweating, and then feeling out of breath. I couldn't breathe. Now, thinking back, it was agonizing. I remember touching my pajamas, and they were wet with sweat. The room was not hot or anything like that. My struggle to breathe lasted for a while longer.

"Then, from not being able to breathe and feeling bad, I went from hot and sweaty to feeling cold. It was a very strange feeling. I didn't like it, although I did not feel any fear. I was very, very cold, and it made me completely immobile. I was paralyzed, up to my neck. I couldn't move. I remember telling myself, 'I hope that this cold goes quickly.' Then it did, it completely went. And I remember feeling a sense of bliss. Profound, profound, profound bliss. I remember very clearly that I even smiled. I remember being there still covered up to my neck with the duvet, and I smiled. I said to myself, 'Now I will be able to sleep really, really well.' And I did. I slept, and then I woke up. I had breakfast. I was feeling fine. Then I hear my iPhone, and I look at it. I saw my sister's name, and I knew. Everything clicked. Immediately I knew that my mother had died. It was mom saying goodbye.

"My sister told me that when they went to wake up my mom, they found her dead. She had died in the night. I have no doubts that it was my mother who came to me. We had so many conversations as well about me being the skeptical one, while she said that she believed that there's a type of life after this. She was going to send me some type of signal saying, 'Hey, I told you, and this is me sending you a signal so as to make sure that you get the message.' I don't know."

Javier eloquently captures the impact his SDE has had on his approach to life and to death. "Has it changed my perspective? Yes, I suppose. I do believe that in life, there are so many dimensions and edges to things. We are limited by our senses and through our senses we can experience some dimensions. I do believe that there are dimensions we're not able to comprehend. I do believe that when we die, the spiritual self, the soul, the energy, whatever you want to call it, will go into a different dimension. There, we don't have the same senses and don't perceive and apprehend the world in the same way as we do in this dimension."

Similar to Lula, Javier has also felt protected by his departed loved ones—and this is an occurrence we have found with other experiencers. Javier told us that it is as if he had a "guardian angel," who watched over and protected him. He remembers the July 7, 2005, Underground bombings in London. Javier was on his way to work and had to leave at eight thirty. He was about to get into the elevator for the Tube station when something persuaded him to ride his bicycle instead. "I went back. I took the bicycle out. Sometimes I think, *How strange*. The timing, it was ten minutes. The bomb exploded near Russell Square. I was going to Leicester Square. I would probably have caught one of the trains that was bombed."

·   ·   ·

The concept of care and of having a "guardian angel" extends be-yond protection from physical danger. We find this in the case of Sonya F., who had two distinct SDEs. For years, Sonya thought of her aunt Ursula as her "spiritual mother." Ursula had come to the United States from Germany at age seventeen and had very little opportunity to receive a formal education. But, Sonya says, "She was the source of most of my books and my library. Just a brilliant woman. She had an amazing soul." The two developed their bond when Ursula visited Sonya's family in California one Christmas when Sonya was fifteen. Although Ursula had her own children, she en-couraged Sonya and supported her. They would write each other letters. "I grew up in a very scientific family," Sonya explains, "and they thought a lot of Ursula's ideas were outlandish." But not Sonya. She turned to her tall, slender aunt, who was always animated and loved to talk with her hands. "By the time I was about nineteen or twenty, we were more like equals. I could go to her for things that I couldn't go to my parents for."

After her own children had "flown the coop," Ursula attended massage school. She moved to Santa Fe, New Mexico, and started working with elderly patients. "When she was about fifty-eight, Ursula was diagnosed with colon cancer," Sonya recalls. "Unfortu-nately, it had metastasized, and it was already in her liver. I knew that likely she wouldn't survive too long, and because of my close-ness to her, I left my home in California to be with her."

Ursula moved in with her daughter and son-in-law, who were both doctors. Sonya found a place nearby. "They were quite busy, and I did a lot of the care and just hanging out with her as much as I could. As she got sicker, I started trying to study how to help her better. I read Sogyal Rinpoche's book, *The Tibetan Book of Living and*

Dying. In the end, I stayed with her all the time." Sonya recalls that it became too painful for her aunt to eat. "She called me one day and said, 'I'm not gonna eat anymore, I'm not gonna drink anymore, so you might as well pack your bags and come over and plan to stay because I'm going now.'

"It was difficult to see someone basically dwindle down. My cousin and I could lift her easily by ourselves to change the pads underneath her sheets. And yet she was still there. I could talk to her and she would raise her hand to answer me. On a Friday night, I started praying for her to be able to go. She was so distressed and agitated. As she got closer to death, I started feeling like my loss was someone else's gain. I can't exactly explain it, but I literally felt like the heavens and all our deceased relatives were celebrating that she would be coming.

"She died around five in the morning. My cousin woke me up, and the two of us prepared her body. I could see her mouth starting to go into a smile and her body stayed warm. The room felt different—it felt like the color of the room had changed, and it felt like the room's size had changed in one corner, as if it had become a cathedral. The best way I can describe it is that the whole atmosphere changed. Then I had this sensation of electrical energy moving through my body. I had the very strong sense that my aunt's spirit had just walked out.

"Eventually, the mortuary staff arrived. When her body was taken away, it was literally like a part of my life had left the room. I remember my cousin saying, 'Do you want to stay for dinner?' And I felt like I had no purpose there anymore. I literally packed my bags and went to the airport without a ticket. When I arrived, I had tears streaming down my face. I said, 'My aunt just died, and I don't have

any need to be here anymore and can you get me on a flight?' It felt
so strong, that sensation of somebody's presence leaving and there
no longer being a purpose to be there. It was like my purpose was
finished. I got on a plane and went back to California."

Sonya adds, "For a while I felt a really strong presence from Ursula after she passed, like she was orchestrating some things in my
life. She used to joke that, 'If you don't meet your husband before I
die, I'm gonna go find him.' I did meet the man that I married right
before she died. We got engaged that year. And had a couple children shortly after getting married. I was forty when I had my first
child. I felt like she was giving me a little push from the other side."

The same year that Sonya's aunt passed away, a friend rec-
ommended that Sonya join a local California women's group.
The group's leader was a woman named Dennie. They met once
a week, and Sonya participated for six months, until she and her
new husband relocated to Massachusetts. "I just always felt this special connection with Dennie. I kind of assumed she had that with
everyone. It wasn't a very long-term relationship, just a very connected one." The two exchanged Christmas cards and sporadically
kept in touch. Then, Sonya recalls, "One of my parents had a medical emergency and I had to fly out to California. I ran into Dennie
in a parking lot. It was before she knew she had cancer. That day, I
recognized that for some reason I always felt like Dennie could see
more of me than I could see of myself. I don't know how to explain
it, but I always felt like she saw my potential, more than I could.
When we left, she said, 'I just want you to know that I'll always love
you.' I thought, 'Dennie will probably say that to anybody,' but still,
it's very special to know that we had that conversation.

"I heard about Dennie being ill and unfortunately I recognized

that she had a fast-moving cancer. I thought, 'Well, I've got a couple months, a few months.' I immediately wrote her a letter, but I
planned on more communication and maybe trying to fly out. Then
I got very busy. I have young kids. It was just kind of one of those
things that gets sidelined. Late one afternoon, I came home after
being at tae kwon do with my children, and I just had this feeling
of sudden, absolute exhaustion. I was literally counting the minutes
until my husband got home from work, just looking at the clock,
thinking, 'I need to sleep. I don't know what this is, but I have to
lie down.'

"My husband got home around seven. At seven thirty I said, 'I
have to lie down.' I didn't even take off my clothes. I slept most of
the night. A sort of dead-to-the-world sleep. Then I started having
a very intense dream. I was on a pontoon boat in a narrow channel.
There were buildings that looked like a combination of what you
would see in Greece with white buildings, and others more fantas-
tical, like out of a Dr. Seuss book, but they were rising out of the
ocean on either side, and the channel was pretty hard to navigate. I
remember turning around and seeing lots of people seated in rows
behind me, and I felt excited. They were all people I was connected
with in some way, even though I couldn't make out a face. I felt like
these are my people, this is my kin that I'm here with.

"It was getting dark. The water was starting to look almost
black. Like what you would see at sundown. I was told that we were
going to head to an airport. And someone said, 'Near New Jersey,'
where I've never been. From there, the scene switched. I stepped
off the boat, and I was on sand. I looked up and this was the most
amazing part. There were crowds of people around me. I looked up,
and there was Dennie looking straight at me.

"I thought, 'Wait a second, Dennie's on this journey? She's sick, this is kind of a hard journey, why is she here?' But she was super excited, and she wanted to go. In front of us was a set of stairs, kind of what you would see at a beach house. They were whitewashed, weathered gray, and they were open. You could see the sand between them. There seemed to be some able-bodied people around. I thought we can all help her go on this journey, but then she looked to me as if to say, 'You can do this, Sonya.' I felt this tremendous responsibility, like, 'Really, me? Why are you picking me? There are all these other people that can help you up these stairs.'

"Dennie wanted to be in the front. We started heading up the stairs, and at one point I looked for signs of her illness, and I thought, 'She just looks kind of tired, and she looked a little jaundiced.' Her skin looked a little dark, and her hands were a little swollen but other than that, she was really cheerful. She was wearing a blue dress, with stripes of cherry-blossom-type flowers. It was flowy and elegant. She had been a dancer, and it was characteristic of what you would see her wear. At one point, she showed me her fingers, and it looked like she was making a V. The first thing that came to mind was, this is a V for victory.

"The stairs seemed like they were endless. I started feeling like we were in the sky. My sense of responsibility was really intense because we would sometimes sort of falter. She would kind of falter, and I'd grab on to her, and I'd feel myself shaking. Like I was responsible for making sure that she didn't fall. I looked up and became aware that there were people waiting for us at the end of the stairs. It was very high. There was no more scenery. I couldn't see any earth, sand, or anything anymore. We were in the sky. And yet I got the sense that we were going to an entrance or a portal leading into a room. The next time I looked up, there were two women in Renaissance dresses, big, poofy, satiny, rust-colored dresses, and they were super excited. They were like, 'She's coming, she's coming.' I started having this feeling that Dennie was the guest of honor. Then I had a sort of selfish feeling that I didn't want to give her up. I recognized she was going to be the center of attention when we got to the top of the stairs. I stopped and rested with her for a while, the idea being, let you rest. But in a way I think that I was hanging on a little longer.

"When we got close enough, they kind of pulled Dennie up into the room. The environment felt almost Middle Eastern. There were pillows and there was going to be a dance performance. Dennie was really happy. She was exhausted, so we got her situated, and for some reason it seemed important that she was leaning up against a wall. Like she wasn't quite capable of sitting up on her own. There was also a sense of waiting; it was as if the timing was off. I can't explain it any other way other than to say that she was early. I had a sense that there was supposed to be a massive spread of food, but it wasn't quite ready. And the dancers weren't quite ready. It was like we were waiting for other people to arrive. Yet I knew it was going to be this amazing, festive thing with this spread of food. Dennie loved beautiful things, and I could just visualize what it was going to be. I could even smell what was coming from the kitchen, but nothing was quite ready.

"When she sat down, she had this beaming face, and she said, 'I made it, I made it.' It was mostly women who were in this room. I think there were a few men, but it was mostly women. Then I started having this sensation of an intense electrical kind of vibration in my body. It was so strong that it felt like it was waking me up, like I was literally being pulled into an upright position off my mattress.

"I knew that I needed to leave that environment because it was the death space or something like that. But at the same time, it was also a really wonderful feeling; it was just bliss. And I didn't want to leave. I suddenly became aware in this dual moment of both knowing that I had to leave but also being desperate to stay because she was dying—and that, when I woke up, I wouldn't be in this amazing place, surrounded by this amazing energy, anymore.

"I woke up literally with tears flying out of my eyes. I was so upset. I actually out loud said, 'Dennie I love you!' I guess I made enough sound that my husband woke up, and he asked, 'What happened?' I said, 'I think Dennie just died.' And I said, 'I just had a dream that felt so much like what it felt like when my aunt died.'

"I got up and wrote the dream down. Then I went on Facebook, and I saw that Dennie's son had posted, *Be with my mom, she's on her journey.* It had been posted hours before."

Sonya has reflected on her experience, and the central question of why she was the one whom Dennie selected to accompany her. "Thinking back, I guess I felt like in a weird way, I was available to help, so she nabbed me. Somehow, thankfully, I was aware enough that I needed to lie down because I think none of this would have happened if I had ignored that and kept going." Instead, Sonya's bliss-like feeling lasted for days.

"There are also strange things that have cropped up," she adds. "About a month after this experience, I got a clothing catalog in the mail; in it was a picture of a brand-new dress, the exact dress I saw in my dream, down to the sleeves that were see-through. I opened the catalog and saw what the model was wearing. It was just so crazy. Strangely, I feel almost closer to Dennie now. I feel her presence a lot. She'll pop into my mind, like an old friend. And sometimes I will get that buzzy energy back in my body."

Sonya describes her own religious life as a mishmash. "I have been a meditator much of my life, but I don't have any particular religious path. I study Kundalini yoga, but then I will do something from Hinduism. I sometimes pray the rosary." But she does believe something exists beyond this current life, although, like many other shared death experiencers, Sonya has shied away from discussing what happened. "The only thing I really shared with my family is that I'm no longer afraid to die, not at all, which is weird. I saw my aunt in quite a bit of pain, but I'm just not afraid. I definitely feel that there's some kind of continuum."

Thus far, we have seen how the shared death experience can deepen existing bonds and connections, as well as be a way for loved ones and friends to be linked to the dying or deceased. In the cases of Lula, Javier, and Sonya, we also see elements of caregiving; a sense among each person that their loved ones have found ways to look after them after death: Lula and her daughter, Felicia; Javier and perhaps his brother; Sonya and her aunt Ursula. But sometimes the care offered to the experiencer is more immediate; it provides closure or repair to a relationship. The SDE itself becomes a source of healing. We will turn to this facet next.

9

UNEXPECTED GIFTS

BRIAN S. was listening to Garrison Keillor's radio show, *A Prairie Home Companion*, as he was driving to a birthday party. "I was listening to his tales from Lake Wobegon, and he was talking about the Tollefson family." At the party, Brian met Kristi. Keillor's fictional Lake Wobegon with its Scandinavian immigrants was in Minnesota; Kristi had grown up on a nine-hundred-acre wheat farm in New Rockford, North Dakota, about four miles outside of town. Kristi and Brian talked for about fifteen minutes before she had to leave. "I never got her number or anything," he recalls. "I just really liked her." Kristi was now living in Southern California; Brian lived and worked in the San Francisco area. "I called Directory Information for Kristi, found her number, and called her up." They met in April, began dating in May, and Brian proposed in August. "It went completely against my nature," he says. "She was Lutheran, she was

Republican, and all these things that I normally wouldn't like, and I always swore I'd live with somebody for a couple of years before I ever asked them to marry me. But none of that mattered, I just fell in love."

Brian describes Kristi, whom he called Kris, as "sincerely interested in everybody that she would meet. She just made people feel really comfortable and cared about." She also had "a wonderful singing voice and was a great musician," who played the piano and trombone. The two played Haydn duets, Kris on the piano and Brian on the oboe, and they would sing Christmas carols. "In terms of both sound and sort of that caring quality, her voice sounded like Julie Andrews's," Brian recalls.

They married and had two children. In 1993, when their daughter was four years old and their son was two, Kris went to the doctor for what she thought was a sinus infection. Instead, "he felt a really big lump in her throat." A round of biopsies and tests ensued. Brian says, "I remember very vividly being at work when we got the results of the biopsies . . . She had what's called papillary thyroid cancer, and it had spread to the lymph nodes in her neck. When I heard that, even though I was in an open area with a lot of people, I just put my head on the desk and cried. Because in my mind, what that meant was she was dead. She was going to die."

Kris underwent a ten-hour surgery. It removed most of the cancer, but also damaged her vocal cords, leaving her unable to sing. Three months later, she had a radioactive iodine treatment designed to kill any of the cells the surgery had missed. "We spent almost five years thinking everything was fine. Every six months, the doctors would do a scan and it would be completely negative." Brian and Kris continued with their lives. "Kris was a marriage and family therapist. She worked with emotionally disturbed adolescents, primarily in the school systems. She worked hard. We were raising our kids." But Kris's blood markers for something called thyroid globulin were slowly rising, which was a concern because she was not supposed to have a thyroid anymore.

Brian recalls, "I was working for Mitsubishi Electric, in their semiconductor division. They had a medical imaging group, and they put me in touch with a Stanford radiologist and a Harvard radiologist. I described what was happening with Kris and I said, 'Are there any developments in imaging technology that might pick up very small amounts of tumor?' The Stanford radiologist put me in touch with a guy who was in the nuclear medicine department, doing PET scanning, which at that time—this is 1997, 1998—was not approved as a means of tracking cancer. But this guy was doing research, and we got special approval. The only place that had a PET scan at that time was the Palo Alto Veterans Administration. Neither Kris nor I is a vet. So, we had to get permission from the state for her to be given a PET scan there."

The scan revealed half a dozen tumors in Kris's lungs and more in her throat. "If we had gone with the assumptions that Kris's doctors were making at the time, she would have died many years earlier," Brian explains. Instead, the couple embarked on years of surgeries. "Probably every eighteen months, she would have surgery on her neck to take out tumors. We always had this attitude of this is tough, but we're going to treat this more like diabetes or some ongoing condition rather than an inevitably fatal disease. And we basically thought we could deal with whatever came up, which was true up until the summer of 2012."

That summer, Kris's condition deteriorated, the tumors began to compromise her lungs, and she struggled to breathe. "We learned on a Tuesday that she was going to pass away very quickly. By that time, she had lost the ability to speak. She could squeeze my hand, so we could communicate somewhat. A big factor was her lung function. She was afraid of suffocating. Sometimes, her body would just panic. We didn't know how to go through this.

"One of the great gifts I got was when one of the ICU nurses suggested that it would be okay for me to lie in bed with Kris and hold her. When I got into bed with her, her lungs weren't going up and down, and her heart wasn't pumping very much. Her blood flow was slowing down and so she felt, to me, like almost wet, lumpy concrete that was hardening. Her body felt cold, but I could tell that the warmth of my body holding her was comforting. She was still agitated until about the last hour before she passed away. After that, there was a distinct feeling of peace that came into Kris, I could feel it in her, and then I could feel it in the room. And it was almost holy. There was a reverent feeling in this."

Brian notes all the ways that he and Kris were different, from their approach to religion to even the amount of emotion they brought to their relationship. "Kris was very grounded. She was very practical. She grew up on a farm with dairy cows; her family worked hard, and they didn't have much money. I am more of a dreamer or something. We would butt heads. In some senses, I was the emotional carrier of the relationship. Usually, that's the woman and not the guy, but it was reversed for me and Kris. That brought up some conflicts, and there are things we did sometimes that really hurt each other; things like that were just stuff of a marriage over several decades."

But as Brian lay there, holding Kris, he had a completely

unexpected sensation. "I'm trying to be sad because even with the hard things, we had a really wonderful relationship, we loved each other dearly. And I start feeling the opposite of sadness, it's a feeling of joy and uplift." He adds, "Kris was lying on my right side, and this feeling is very distinctly coming from the right side into me." He thought he could be grieving, but instead he felt "the resolution of every issue we ever had. Every dispute was just simply settled somehow." Brian also stresses that these differences did not simply dissolve; rather they were fully resolved. "I still can't get my mind around that. I don't understand how that happened. But it was this clear, clear experience. It was an experience of her loving me and being with me forever, and me loving her and being with her forever."

In that hospital room, Brian and Kris's son was having a hard time facing his mother's death. He rested his head on his father, and Brian was periodically aware of both of his children and was concerned about them. "But as soon as I thought about them, it cut off this experience I was having. So I learned to just be with Kris. She would take a breath and then minutes would go by and I would think, 'Oh, this is it. She's gone.' But then there'd be another breath. And I'm lying there just feeling this joy and uplift." Brian also had a profound sensation of what he calls "an expanded presence and large beingness." He could sense the separate identities of Kris and their children in the room, but at the same time he was very aware of something much greater than the three-dimensional world that we live in. "The only way I can explain it is that we cram ourselves down in this three-dimensional body, but actually our beings are much more dimensional in ways my mind could not comprehend—and Kris was now in these extra dimensions. I was

lying there, feeling her being as big and huge and loving and powerful and uplifting.

"Eventually, she did stop breathing and the nurse came in and
pronounced her dead. I think we got out of the hospital about four
thirty in the morning on a Thursday. I started driving home, and
I come over a hill, and there's this huge full moon. It was almost
orange, and it turned out it was a blue moon, so that was amazing."

Brian says ever since that night, he has carried with him the
particular sense of what he felt from Kris. "I was expecting that I
was going to be really sad and full of grief. But I couldn't hold that
because the joy and the uplift and the sense of this huge 'beingness'
that she was, that was taking precedence. All those petty little things
that our minds put in the way of just having our heart open and loving . . . this experience with Kris in those final hours had the power
to remove those things. Over time, I've interpreted it as a moment
of divine grace."

Brian's intense emotion is not unique. Others who have had
a shared death experience have also found that an SDE can create
lasting healing in a relationship. Elizabeth B. was living in France in
1991 while she was pregnant with her second child. "My husband is
French, so we had moved to France. I had a very difficult pregnancy.
I was on an IV for two months. Chelsea, my daughter, was born at
six and a half months, and she survived for two days on a respirator.
I came home from the hospital, and my saving grace was having my
son, Morgan, there. I know that he aided me in healing from that
passing.

"I think that for anyone who has had either a miscarriage or
had a child die right after childbirth . . . it's very, very difficult. The
thing that kept me going was that I needed to get up and running

immediately for Morgan. Second, I knew that it was possible to have more children, and I was very, very fortunate. I have two beautiful daughters who were born after Chelsea passed away.

"But after losing Chelsea, I felt as if I had one foot here and one foot over there. I felt like we were going to be together again ultimately, and that in part she was always with me." The depth of that feeling shifted after Morgan attended an exchange program with thirteen other students in Nanjing, China.

"He had a school break, and one option was for him to visit some friends in Hong Kong. My husband had worked there, and he and I were very concerned that if Morgan went to Hong Kong, he might not get back into China. He had a special type of student visa that allows for leaving China, but you're never really sure that you're going to be admitted back in. Then he told us that all of the students were going to Tibet. Two professors were going to be traveling with the group, so we thought it would be wonderful for him to have this opportunity. He landed in Lhasa [Tibet's capital], which is at eleven thousand feet altitude, with all of the other students, but not the professors, who had decided not to go. Unfortunately, they immediately decided to go the next day to the base camp for Mount Everest, which is at nineteen thousand feet. As they made the trip up, everybody in the bus was sick. Girls were throwing up, and Morgan was holding their heads. He had spent time in China before, and so he was kind of everyone's big brother.

"By the time that they got to the base camp," Elizabeth continues, "everybody was so sick. They were urinating on themselves in the bus. Nobody understood that this was a symptom of altitude sickness and they didn't understand that these were really serious signs. Morgan went to bed early because he had a terrible migraine.

During the night, he kept getting up and wandering aimlessly and calling the other students by the wrong name. At nine in the morning, they tried to wake Morgan up, and he was foaming at the mouth, and they couldn't wake him up.

"One student has a mother who's a medical doctor. He called her on his cell phone, and she said that it was really important to get him down to a lower altitude immediately. They loaded him onto the bus. He was a big guy, six foot six, two hundred eighty pounds. They started down the mountain, and he stopped breathing. They got him off the bus to try to do CPR on him, but none of the kids really knew how to do CPR. The director of the program in Nanjing had been told what was going on, and he called me in Arizona with the phone number of Morgan's roommate, Colin, and told me that if I'd like to, I could call Colin.

"I immediately called, and what's so nice about Colin is that he didn't mince words. He told me, 'Morgan is not doing well. I don't think he's going to make it. He's undergoing CPR, but he's not breathing.' I asked Colin to put the phone up to Morgan's ear, and I told Morgan that we were proud of him, that we loved him and not to be afraid."

Elizabeth describes the response: "It was instantaneous; he hugged me from the inside. Morgan was thousands of miles away, but I felt it immediately. I'm not religious. As I say, I'm spiritual. I'd never had something like this happen before, but I knew immediately that first of all, Morgan will always be with us. I knew that love never dies, and I felt incredibly connected to Morgan. Then my husband said, 'Let me speak to him,' because he didn't even realize from the tone of my voice and what I was saying that Morgan had passed away.

"I said in French, 'Honey, I'm sorry. I think he's gone.' It was a very, very hard thing for my whole family because I don't think that they were immediately able to experience the same thing as I was experiencing."

But Elizabeth has carried this experience with her ever since. She explains, "I'm in contact with Morgan all the time. When he lived in China or even when he was down in Tucson, I had to depend on a telephone to talk to him, and we often spoke twice a day. Now I feel that whenever I need him, he's there with me. I wouldn't say that I necessarily talk to him, although I talk to him out loud a lot, but I do feel him with me all the time.

"I haven't ever really cried from Morgan's passing. He's my firstborn. He's my boo-boo. He's the love of my life. But I was never able to cry because every time that I started thinking of him and feeling sad, I would then feel this kind of welling up of wonderful energy inside of me, as though I was being hugged from the inside. I still get hugged from the inside, especially, for instance, if I'm down about something else, if I'm concerned about something else that's happening in my life, I'll feel him hug me.

"My two daughters will say, 'Mom, being hugged from the inside sounds so weird. You need to figure out a different way of explaining that,' but that feeling is what it is. For me, it comes from my belly all the way up through my heart and it just doesn't allow me to be sad anymore. It fills me. It's just a huge sense of peace, and it brings joy as well.

"Probably about a month after he passed, I had a really beautiful dream about Morgan. It took place in Jamaica, where we had gone for one of our last family trips together. He walked up to me in a market and hugged me and told me that everything was going to be okay and then walked off. I expected to get lots more hugs like that. I haven't, but it's still okay. One of the things that I think everybody needs to understand, and I believe this happens in my own life, is that we actually spend a lot of time with our loved ones while we're asleep, and we don't necessarily remember the dreams. I always wake up happy, and I'm pretty sure that I'm spending time with Morgan and Chelsea over there."

Elizabeth was also determined to use this experience to reach out to others. "The first thing that I wanted to do was to connect with other parents whose children had passed because I realized this must happen with everyone because our love for our children is so profound. I know that the reason I was able to connect with Morgan was because he wanted to let me know that he was okay. He wanted to let me know that everything was going to be okay with us as well. I tried a lot of grief groups, and none of them spoke about a connection with our children in the afterlife. As a matter of fact, it was taboo in the groups that I was able to find.

"I also wanted to see what other parents were like one year down the line, two years down the line, six years down the line, and their families too, and if this is something that you can survive. Now, almost nine years down the line, I realize that you cannot only survive, but you can experience joy again. You can thrive."

Elizabeth ultimately started a group named Helping Parents Heal. She explains, "One of the main points of the group is that we now call ourselves 'shining light parents.' It's not that we're shining, it's because our kids are shining through us, and they do. They shine through us and they actually show us the way to heal." She adds, "I don't think that I am unique at all. There's nothing unique about me. I think that everyone can be in contact with their loved ones. I was just lucky in terms of the rapidity with which it happened with Morgan, because of the fact that I already had one foot here and one foot on the other side with Chelsea. But I don't think that anyone should feel badly if it doesn't happen immediately when their loved ones pass. At the same time I think that anyone who does have this happen should realize that it's also very normal.

"We're all just experiencing different degrees of the same thing, which is an enormous outpouring of love. All of this comes from love, the love that Morgan and I shared, the love that I share with Chelsea as well, and now the love that I share with all of these other parents. One of the main things that we talk about in our group is that our children are home, and we're still in 'school.' We've still got something to learn here. We're still here for a reason, but they want us to be happy, and they want us to experience joy, because they're happy, they're joyful. That's a very important thing for people to understand. The children accomplished what they needed to do while they were here. In many cases, I believe that a lot of these kids are very, very old souls. They got what they needed to do done, and now they're over there. Another thing that we talk about in our group, and I totally believe, is that when we do see our kids again, it will be as though not one minute has passed because time is completely different over there from the way that it is here."

Like many shared death experiencers, Elizabeth says, "You totally, totally don't fear death and dying, but that's with a caveat: No one needs to speed the process up. We do have a role here on earth." And she believes very deeply that bereaved parents should not feel alone. Instead, parents who have already experienced this kind of loss can "reach a hand back to another parent to help pull them forward."

For both Brian and Elizabeth, a shared death experience strengthened a long-term relationship and, in the case of Brian, also helped to repair accumulated abrasions in his marriage. But what about significantly frayed relationships, or challenged relationships, where the shared bonds have been damaged seemingly irreparably? Can they also be transformed? In some cases, the answer is yes. Julie S. describes herself as "a skeptic by nature. I don't believe in ghosts. I've never had a 'psychic' experience. As a nurse, I have seen patients die and have comforted families, but I had never heard of a shared death experience, much less had one."

Julie's story starts with a phone call from her grown daughter, Sophie. She explains, "Sophie's father and I had divorced a lifetime ago, when she was nine years old and her sister and brother were seven and five. It wasn't the best marriage, and we did not have an easy divorce. I moved on, got my nursing degree, and eventually happily remarried. My ex also remarried, and by the time Sophie called, he and I had been out of contact for about a decade."

From her kids, Julie knew that her ex-husband had been confined to a wheelchair for several months and that he was in the early stages of dementia. Although he was only in his sixties, he required constant care and had been moved to a nursing home. Julie recalls that it was a brutally hot weekend, with a high of 104 degrees. But her daughter Sophie asked to come visit and to bring her own daughters. When Julie asked why, Sophie answered that she had woken up that morning and thought she should.

Next, Julie recalls, "On the way into town, Sophie stopped at the nursing home to visit her dad. They walked in his room, the girls called out, 'Hi, Grandpa!' and then they all froze. He was unresponsive." Sophie called for help. Her father's blood pressure had dropped to 75/45. His pulse was 133. "When Sophie told me what had happened, I knew it was serious.

"I said, 'If you want to say goodbye to your dad, this is the time.'

"Finally, everyone came back home. We made a plan for the next day and decided that I'd take the girls to the movies. They had said their goodbyes, and Sophie would then be free to stay at the bedside. In the morning after breakfast, Sophie went back to the nursing home, and the girls and I went to the movies."

About halfway through the movie, Julie had what she describes as "a distracting impression" and felt a sensation that, "Something's happening. His condition is changing. He's going.

"I pushed the thought away as imagination, but it stayed and was hard to ignore, like when my dog stares at me silently with his big eyes. I was being asked to do something, and in my spirit, I hesitated, but then said yes." What happened next was transformative. Julie explains, "I closed my eyes and time and space changed. I was with him in this new space. The movie screen and sounds completely were gone."

Julie describes seeing her ex-husband "wrapped like a mummy, with only his head uncovered. His features were not clear, like an image in an old mirror and with a sepia filter. The outer layers of fabric around his form were loose and flowing, a linen-like material but more flowy. It had no end; the fabric just merged into the dark background space around him.

"He was moving upward to the light above his head. I looked at it." She recalls seeing "a beautiful, diffuse light that was more than light. It was a place, a space, an energy. It was freedom and release and forgiveness and acceptance." She felt that "I was glimpsing eternity."

In that moment, Julie heard him "saying, 'I have to go. I can't hang on,' not in voice or words," she adds, but instead expressed "clearly and to me. More clear than voice or words, it was a knowing. Then I understood I was there to help him pass. He had to go, and somehow I was part of it. I sent my energy to help propel his spirit upward. To pass. I told him, 'It's good, yes, go. Go in peace.'"

Julie says, "It was the most profound, indescribable, and most peaceful feeling I have ever, ever experienced. Then, it was over." Julie's attention returned to the movie and the smell of popcorn. She recalls thinking, "Did this just happen? Have I imagined it all?" Her next thoughts were, "No one would believe me, and I wasn't sure I believed it.

"I needed to know the time. I reached inside my purse for my phone. It was 1:32.

"I decided to text my daughter." Julie thought about asking if "your dad just died," but instead she wrote, *Weird Feeling.* Sophie responded immediately, *I think he just died.*

"*I know*, I texted back. *I felt it.*" In that moment, Julie says, "I realized how hard this was going to be to tell anyone. It transcended words." She adds, "I was humbled that somehow I was chosen or allowed to witness his passing."

Later, Sophie told her mom that in her father's last moments, "He opened his eyes just before he died, and his lips moved." To which, Julie says, "I thought, 'Yes, I know,'" adding, "To glimpse eternity as a mere mortal, the whole thing brought me to my spiritual knees." Julie says that this experience has left her "less skeptical and not afraid of death." And she hopes her story helps others and "gives comfort."

Similar to the deep emotions and resolutions felt by both Brian

and Elizabeth, Julie found that her ex-husband's transition and passing produced a feeling of profound peace. Although she encountered
less of an overt physical sensation than either Brian or Elizabeth did,
her experience relates back to prior SDEs we have encountered,
where the recipient acted as a guide and felt the sensation of rising
up and sharing in an "energetic" departure. This range of experiences also underscores to us as researchers that there is no "right
way" to experience an SDE, nor do the elements of an SDE deter-
mine its immediate and subsequent impact on the experiencer. In
fact, as we have repeatedly seen, the power of the SDE is in many
ways independent of its elements. This finding is particularly appar-
ent when different individuals participate in a single SDE.

As a researcher and a therapist, one of the most fascinating
aspects that I have encountered is the "multiple" SDE, where two
people in the same room experience the passing of a loved one.
One example of this was captured in Scott T.'s recounting of Nolan's
passing, where his girlfriend, Mary Fran's sister, was in another part
of the room and also experienced an SDE. Now we will explore this
in more depth with two cases, one from London and another from
California.

10

SHARING THE SHARED
DEATH EXPERIENCE

LARRY C. was known as "Mr. Santa Barbara," although he was born in Massachusetts in 1923 and grew up in Newark, New Jersey. His family lost everything during the Great Depression, which drove Larry's father to the breaking point. "His mother went to work as a shoe salesclerk, had multiple jobs, and was taking care of her three sons and her husband," recalls Larry's youngest child, Leslie. The caregiving for her husband was particularly difficult; my grandmother would "tie her husband to her arm at night with a towel." Otherwise, he had a tendency to get up and "wander around the neighborhood. Sometimes Dad would be sent out to look for his father if he had wandered off," Leslie explains.

Larry enlisted in the army in 1943 and became a bombardier in the Army Air Corps. Although he was awarded a Purple Heart, in the beginning, "he liked to say that he was one of the worst bombardiers in history," Leslie jokes. "He was supposed to bomb Vienna, and he hit the lever too early and all the bombs dropped into a lake, thirty miles outside of the city. Since his plane was the lead in the formation, the other twenty dropped their bombs too early as well." Larry returned home, attended Syracuse University, and ended up in New York City. "He had a job with the telephone company for a while, as a telephone technician, which was a scream to me. If you know my dad, he was so technically disinclined he struggled to make toast."

But he loved to dance. Larry found a job as a professional ball-room dance instructor at an Arthur Murray Dance Studio. There, he met his future wife, Marcy, and also caught the eye of Arthur Murray, who sent the pair around the country to help open additional Murray Dance Studios. In California, they were given a choice between relocating to Santa Barbara or Bakersfield. "My mom went to Bakersfield, burned her hand on the car door, and said, 'I am not bringing up my children here.' So they moved to Santa Barbara.

"Throughout their whole marriage, and when times were the worst and they were the most irritated with each other, dancing was the magic elixir because it was the one thing they couldn't do without the other. And they also couldn't do it with any other person. On the dance floor," Leslie recalls, "my father was like butter, smooth as silk." She remembers watching her parents leave for an evening out, her father dressed in a tuxedo and her mother in a ball gown. "They were beautiful. They looked like they were going to Cinderella's ball at Disneyland."

Larry was also a sought-after emcee for charity events. "He had this big barrel chest and would light up a room just by walking into it," Leslie says, but even more, he had an "ability to transcend social boundaries. He was as comfortable with Ronald Reagan and five-million-dollar donors as he was with the fry cooks in the back. In fact, he was more comfortable with the fry cooks because that's where he came from. But he just had this magical ability with people. His greatest gift was connecting with people where they were and making them feel seen and appreciated and known. He was genuinely interested in what you had to say. What was your history? That kind of authenticity of interest is so rare. Most of us barely have it for our small circle of loved ones, but he had it for everyone."

Family life at home was not perfect, although Leslie does have fond memories. She was the youngest of five children, "the caboose in a big Catholic family," as she puts it. Her mother was incredibly busy. Of her father, she says, "He may have been a less-than-perfect husband in terms of helping around the house or helping with the childcare, but he was the World's Greatest Dad. And he was always ready to take you to sports or run around the yard or play word games. When my mom would get angry at him, she'd say, 'I have six children.'"

Then the first of many tragedies struck. Two days before Leslie's birthday and as she was preparing to graduate from Stanford University, her older sister committed suicide. "She was fourteen years older and the absolute light of my life, and it was a crushing blow to the family. She was kind of a second mom to everyone. There was Ashley and my three brothers and me. The two of us were very close, unusual for a teenager and a young adult; she would send me little trinkets or cards or whatever and bring me gifts and spend time with me. We would go on adventures, and she would take me to the Museum of Natural History and for lunch, or we'd go looking at shells on the beach with a magnifying glass and a book that had all of the scientific names, and we'd figure out which ones were which and how they fit together.

"We had this storybook relationship, and then about three or four years before her death, she started to have some symptoms of depression. By the end, she was in such pain. I remember my brother Michael calling me and saying, 'Hey, we're coming up to get you.' And I asked, 'Why?' It was so hard for me, and I cannot imagine what it was like for my parents to lose a child.

"We were not a family that talked a lot about how we felt except to say, 'I love you.' I just remember my parents would go in their room and shut the door, which they never did during the day, and grieve, I think because they didn't want us to see them cry. We all did our grieving privately. My mother would occasionally say, 'How are you doing with this?' But there wasn't a huge amount of talking about the loss. It was more you try to rub someone's shoulders or bring them a glass of tea or do something nice for them or say, 'Oh, why don't we go for a walk?' or whatever. I was a competitive athlete in basketball, and I think I talked a few times to our team psychologist, but it was definitely more of 'How do you get tools to deal with this?' In the same way that I would ask a plumber, 'What do I buy in the hardware store to fix this sink?'

"My father was quite a verbal genius, and his way of coping ultimately was to talk to his friends and talk about the experience in public. And my mother was at the exact opposite end of the spectrum. Very, very private. My parents were complete opposites in many ways, and by the time I came along, I don't know that they had a lot in common besides the family. They had very different styles of living, and there was some resentment. My mother resented that my dad spent so much time in the community and then would come home and not participate. And my dad resented that she wasn't more supportive of what he did, although for years they were out doing community activities together four or five nights a week."

Leslie enrolled in graduate school at Stanford, played on an NCAA championship basketball team, and ultimately spent three years playing professional ball in Japan, at a time when there was no women's professional leagues in the United States. She inherited her love of basketball from her dad. "My mother took us to church. Dad may have come once or twice, but he usually played basketball on Sunday mornings. That was his church, the church of basketball." She returned home when her father suffered a major heart attack. "He pulled, as usual, a rabbit out of the hat and was fine after a five- or six-way bypass." But Leslie decided to stay in California. "I was quite aware that my parents were older. They were forty when they had me. I thought, 'Wow, time is finite, maybe more finite than I think, and I want to be there.'"

She took a job as an assistant basketball coach for the men's team at Westmont, a local college. A freak accident on a recruiting trip left her with a devastating spinal injury and temporarily disabled. "My parents just basically said, 'You're coming back home and we'll take care of you.'" Leslie's mom was her primary caregiver—she had coped with her own serious back injury before Leslie was born and had delivered Leslie while in a full body cast, with a cutout for her abdomen. But Leslie also experienced some special moments with her father. "When I was a little girl, we belonged to a swim club. He would get in the shallow end in four or five feet of water, squat down, and let me stand on his thighs. Then he would hold my hands and walk backward and forward and sing this silly, made-up song, 'Surfer, surfer, when you surf out the door.' Fast-forward twenty years, to one of the first days that that they put me in the water from the wheelchair; he was standing beside the physical therapist in the water with me. He said, 'Come here. Sit on my lap.' So I sat on his legs and we did the same thing. It was this incredible moment of sweetness and tenderness."

Leslie returned to competitive sports, joining a dragon boat team and training for the World Championships. She was also working. Her parents seemed fine; her mother swam a mile a day. "Nobody expected Mom to die first." But at age eighty-three, she suffered a massive stroke and passed away. "Dad said, 'You need to be here because I can't do all of this.' And so I came home, and it was a big relief for him. But as the years passed, part of the problem was that I had inherited Mom's role, but I wasn't Mom."

Leslie's father's own health was declining too; he developed diabetes but still insisted on drinking sugary soda and eating unhealthy foods. "If it had to do with his health or my brothers' health, then I would be just as much a stick in the mud as my mom was, because it was important. I made a choice very early on that I would rather be unpopular than go to funerals. So I was willing to sacrifice the relationship for that, and I did. Our relationship became acrimonious, and he kicked me out." The siblings found a caretaker, and Leslie moved to Oregon to race and later coach dragon boats, winning a world championship.

"I would call my dad periodically. He never called me, but he was not much of a caller anyway. He was an in-person kind of guy. I'd also send him email, jokes and stuff. Sometimes he'd email me, but it felt like he really didn't want anything to do with me for the most part. But I knew he still loved me, and I still loved him. The blessing and the enormous gift of our family is that bedrock of love. It is so deep that you have the freedom to be pissed at somebody, even for years. But if something happens, you drop everything to go show up and help."

After Leslie's father moved to a retirement community, his health noticeably declined. "There was never a question that I would show up when he got sick, even though I was coaching the US Dragon Boat Team at the time and we were in the run-up for the world championships in Russia. I took a leave of absence. Initially, I thought I would be down for a week, and then it became clear that he wasn't going to get better, and I wasn't going to leave.

"One of my dear friends is a palliative-care social worker. I called her, and she mapped the whole thing out for us. These are the different ways it can go, these are the decisions you want to make, and so forth. That was hugely useful, and I think it helped all of us make the best decisions on my dad's behalf.

"Also, having dealt with pain for a significant part of my life, and having been in that hospital bed pushing the call button, you start to recognize the cues and the little tells of 'Okay, the meds are wearing off, it's time for more,' or 'Okay, there's too much now.' He was having trouble sleeping because of the pain; the only way he could sleep was in a chair."

Leslie's father entered hospice care. He began seeing images of his mother—"his mother was very, very dear to him. And he talked about her in angelic terms through his whole life"—and sleeping more and more. "He would start a sentence and then trail off and fall asleep. But the morning before he went into the coma, he had a bounce-back. He wanted to go down and eat breakfast. This was a guy that had trouble walking to the bathroom, his legs were in so much pain. But we went downstairs, and we had breakfast at one of the tables out under the skylight. He had a full breakfast, and he was reading the newspaper, and it reminded me so much of when I was growing up, and he'd eat breakfast and read the newspaper. I remember being grateful that it was a sunny day and he said, 'Oh, it's so nice to be sitting here.' He was quite lucid and alert. And then he said, 'I'm tired, let's go back up.'

"Once he got into bed, he never got up again. I sat with him and read, and my brothers also came to visit. A couple of times, he woke up and smiled or said a sentence and then he'd go back to sleep. But we knew he liked talking and we knew he liked music, so we would sing to him too.

"I was in charge of a one-hundred-fifty-person dragon boat team that was going to the world championships. It was pretty clear that I was letting a lot of people down, but it was never a question for me to leave. On the last morning, two of my brothers were there, and we were sitting around laughing and singing and telling stories, and then they left to pick up sandwiches for lunch. Sarah, my niece, showed up. She and my dad had always been close. She was holding his hand and talking about the good old days. She has this super-sunny personality that Dad really gravitated toward.

"What I remember is that the sun was shining, and Sarah and I were chatting, a little teary-eyed too, because his breathing was slowing, and it seemed like the end was close. I told him, 'This is great, Dad. Sarah is here and she loves you,' and tried to open the space for whatever he needed. Over and over again, all of us had talked to Dad about saying goodbye, and that it was okay to leave whenever he needed to. We had learned that as part of my mom's passing. We said, 'Whenever you need to go, Dad, we're here, we're with you. Totally on your time.'

"Then, all of a sudden, we heard the birds at the window, and they were *so* loud. We never saw them, we only heard them. It was like they were trying to get Dad's attention and he wasn't wearing his hearing aids, so they had to be loud. Sarah and I looked at each other, like, 'What is that?' And then Dad opened his eyes, and he looked toward the window and he smiled. It was that beatific—his brow that had been furrowed was relaxed. He smiled, and then he was gone.

"Sarah said, 'Wow. I think the birds came to get him. I think they were there to say, 'It's okay.' My first thought was, I felt bad that my brothers weren't there. And then, as I was looking toward the window, I had this image of this golden light and Dad with his two brothers and his mom and their arms around each other, walking away, and he was looking back over his shoulder, like, *Yeah, it's okay. I'm good.* They were all young, and he was wearing his army uniform. It was interesting because the pictures that we have of his mother are all from when she's older. I remember that it struck me that I didn't know if I ever saw a picture of her at that age, but there she was. He always described her as being very careworn because of the multiple jobs and the economic stress. But she didn't look careworn, she looked healthy and happy. Dad had his arm around his brother Martin on one side and his mother on the other. And his brother Sam was on the other side, but they were all arm in arm, the four of them walking away. The whole scene was just like a movie, where there's this gold light, not super bright, but you could see it's brighter there, and everybody's smiling and happy and there was a message of *Okay, it's time to go.*

"Dad used to say, 'I'm an atheist who prays.' But in his last six months or so, sometimes he would talk about God, and what it would be like to go to Heaven. I remember him asking me once, 'What do you think it's going to be like?' He would talk about how he looked forward to seeing his mother again. He would say, 'I don't know if all that God stuff you have is right, but if it is, she's in Heaven for sure, and it'll be great to see her because she'll be peaceful. She won't be worried about things. She'll be happy, she'll be taken care of.'

"And I would tease him and say, 'Dad, how do you know you're going?' And he'd answer, 'Oh, I'm going.' I don't think he was sure at all, but we would joke about it."

Leslie works in information technology and operations, and she brings that orientation to her interpretation of this moment around her father's passing. "I am a literal, objective, data-driven person. After I experienced this, I read studies and descriptions of what scientists and people who study these events think is actually happening? There are people who hold the spiritual side as being possible, and there are also a lot of people that don't, who are very reductionist, and say it's just physical. So that makes me aware of the possibility that it's what I had for breakfast, and past images of my father, and things that he said and so forth, coalescing into a story. That's how our brains work. I understand that. But my sense is that's not what it was. Instead, it was a vision, a gift from God or the spiritual realm."

Leslie is also keenly aware that others may dismiss her experience, or at a minimum say that it was a product of the circumstances, generated by her own mind rather than some outside force. Having a scientific, analytical background, she asked those questions of herself. "My strong sense is that it's not just a bunch of neurotransmitters in my brain creating some picture that I imagined, but instead that it was something that actually happened. And I was watching it happen—I was watching his transition back into the arms of his family, which he had been hoping for, and back into youth, which he had been hoping for and talked about a lot. A transition into freedom from the weights of this world and the pain of this period.

"I just loved him," she adds. "He was a great guy and I was blessed to have him as a father, and I wanted him to be out of pain and happy and where he wanted to be. And it looked like he got there."

Sitting with Leslie during that late morning was her niece Sarah, who had her own memories and her own shared death experience with her grandfather's passing. While Leslie was raised by her mother in the Catholic Church, Sarah had grown up with a more wide-ranging religious experience. She describes her relationship with her grandfather by saying, "Out of all the grandchildren, I probably spent the most time with him. I'm sure he made all of us feel like we were his favorite, but after I had my own children, we lived a block away from his house. I would go over all the time and sit with him. I'd come over while he was watching the Lakers and make sure his nails were okay and that his feet were okay because he had diabetes. He always wanted his feet and his hands massaged. We would go to lunch every Tuesday at noon and share a Reuben sandwich. I would try to have them serve him food without french fries, and it was always a battle."

She had her own view of the family dynamics: "He was incredibly close with his mother. He knew to the minute, pretty much, when she had passed. As he was getting closer to the end, he had many dreams about his mother. Anytime he was a bit out of it, immediately he would be reaching for his mother and calling for her and talking. We couldn't make out all of the things that he would say, but it was clear he had been waiting to see her."

However, Sarah's conversations around the afterlife with her grandfather differed from her aunt's. For years, he said that "he did not believe in God at all and was adamant: 'When I die, I die. There will be nothing on the other side.' He also said that he wanted to come back. He wished that he could have faked his death so that he could come back and be there at the funeral, because everyone would be saying such good things about him."

As his health declined, "he was in a ton of pain. He had diabetes, and part of his feet were dying. They were turning black and he was really uncomfortable. By the end, he wanted to be around everyone much, much more because also he wasn't remembering that he had just seen us. He was incredibly irritated because he was desperately trying to talk. I mean, here's a man who wants to talk all the time. Wants to have the floor all the time, and you can see that he was desperate to convey messages."

On that final morning, Sarah recalls, "We had the window open, and the birds were so loud. It went from being very quiet, and I remember asking Les, 'Is it just me?' And she's like, 'No, this is it. We're really experiencing this right now.' We saw him lift his head, smile, take his last breath, and go up. Leslie and I were looking at each other in shock because the birds went crazy.

"We were able to really experience his passing and experience it in a way that he himself did. I think he was probably surprised. He didn't expect to see his mom. Even though I knew that she probably was the most important person in his life, he was not counting on seeing anybody. So, to realize that he was seeing people was incredibly uplifting, to even think that he could reconnect with someone who loved him so much was powerful."

Sarah says she still struggles for the words to fully describe what happened. "I've never experienced anything like the birds. I don't think I've ever heard birds so beautiful. It truly makes you question things a bit. The link that we all have. The months and days leading up to it were so painful. And then when it happened, it was almost like euphoria. Like, 'Oh my gosh, that was gorgeous, didn't expect that to be so beautiful.' I didn't expect to be so happy. I definitely wasn't expecting to feel so joyous. Just hearing the birds and seeing him clearly seeing something on the other side. It was a feeling of, oh, this other step, it finally came. He's there.

"In the end, I felt like he didn't have anything to hang on to. He was like, 'Yeah, that was done. I did it. And on to the next.' I think with my grandmother, she wasn't as prepared for death, whereas he had been saying goodbye for months. The process of being there and experiencing it was healing. If I had just gotten a phone call and I hadn't experienced the beauty of it, things would have been different. I think so many times that with death, there's this shame or a reluctance to talk about it, or that if you say it was beautiful, it's weird or whatever. But for me, being there, I got to experience something sacred and beautiful. I think it was helpful."

But it has been very hard for Sarah to discuss her experience with others, even with her own family. "It almost felt a bit taboo to really discuss it. Some people don't know how to handle death. My mom didn't say much beyond 'Okay, all right.'" As for her feelings of joy, Sarah adds, "I don't think people really wanted to hear about that, to be honest. It was more, are you going to be okay? Reassure us you're going to be okay. People would say, 'You're okay? You're good? Can we bring you flowers? Okay? Are you fine?' because they're uncomfortable. My friend who is the most willing to talk about it is a psychologist, who worked in a cancer ward."

Sarah says the entire experience has led her to rethink her own approach to death. "Looking back now, I think we tried to hold on too long. Part of me wishes we had seen the signs earlier. There was too much medical intervention, all the drugs, the pacemaker. I think if I could have gone back and done anything different, it would have been to have more awareness of the process, asking are we fighting to hold on for us, or is he fighting to hold on for him? Why are we all fighting to make sure he eats his three meals a day if he's not hungry anymore? Every time he went to the hospital, he lost a part of himself. Every time he left the hospital, he was a different person. How long do we need to keep someone here just because we're all so uncomfortable to make that transition?

"I do believe," she adds, "that there is life after. More so than I did before."

In Leslie and Sarah's experiences, we have a powerful demonstration of how a shared death experience can be profoundly similar for two people yet contain key differences. Unlike Scott T.'s case, where both he and his girlfriend's sister had a bedside SDE, but neither was in that moment aware of the other, both Leslie and Sarah were deeply aware that they were jointly sharing in the moment of Larry's passing. They both heard the intense birdsong, saw their father and grandfather raise his head and smile, and felt a flood of peaceful, joyous feelings flow through them, feelings that persisted even during their subsequent period of grief. Leslie's experience included an extra step, the clear vision of her father departing with his mother and brothers, but the ultimate impact on both women was the same. Cases like this are part of the reason why our research suggests very strongly that the existence of the SDE and the ability to perceive it are the key components of the experience, rather than whether an SDE possesses a range of complex elements. SDEs do not need to be grand or showy events to have deep meaning.

Shared SDEs also reveal another "gift," an inadvertent one. Having a shared experience helps give the event increased validity. Scott T. became more certain of what he had experienced after hearing about another experience in Nolan's hospital room. In the case of Leslie and Sarah, each was able to immediately "check in" with the other about the validity and the similarity of what they had experienced. In the next case that we will explore, this act of sharing in a shared death experience helps Amelia B. be more certain of and preserve her own bedside experience.

Amelia is a lawyer, what the British refer to as a solicitor, in the United Kingdom, and the mother of four children. Her third child, Tom, a bright-blond, blue-eyed boy, was diagnosed with a rare cancer, DSRCT, one month after he turned ten. At age eight, Tom would playfully tell her that he was going to die before her and that he would die young. "He just chanted, night after night. 'I'm going to die before you, Mum. I'm not going to grow old. I won't grow old. I'm going to die before you.' And I would just go, 'Don't be silly, obviously I'm going to die before you. I'm ancient.' And he goes, 'No, no, I'm going to die before you,' and very happy about it. It was a bit like Peter Pan, to the point where I phoned up one of my best friends who is a teacher and said, 'I'm really worried. He keeps saying he's going to die before me.' And she said, 'Oh, he's probably watching a film or reading something,' because that was all before any cancer sign.

"When he first was diagnosed, he was a little boy; he liked SpongeBob SquarePants. I remember a few months before he got cancer, he dressed up as SpongeBob with his friend on Halloween night. He never tried to be cool. He didn't have to be a ghoul. He was SpongeBob; he'd wander around all these houses saying 'SpongeBob!' He made up a whole imaginary world with cartoon characters. He had a sort of quirky sense of humor, and he used to keep us grounded and kept us together."

Amelia remembers the exact sequence of events when Tom was first diagnosed. She was divorced from Tom's dad, Chris, and had gotten remarried to a doctor. "He'd been staying with his dad for Easter weekend, and then Tom and his sisters, Anna and Izzy, came back on Easter Monday. His sister Izzy came straight up to me and said, 'Tom's got a lump on his tummy and we've been giving him lots of fruit, but it's still there.' And I remember we were all out in the garden, and it was a sunny day. So I said to my husband now, Tom's stepfather, 'They say Tom's got a lump on his tummy, go and feel it.' He said, 'It's odd.' And he gave my older daughter, Anna, some money and said, 'Go to Waitrose and buy as many laxatives as you can, because it's odd. There's a lump there, just buy every laxative you can.'

"We sort of pumped him with laxatives, but nothing changed.

My husband said, 'I think it might be a lymphoma.' I didn't even know what lymphoma was." Amelia took Tom to the doctor. "That was one of the worst moments. He's lying on the bed and the doctor, who I vaguely know socially, just looked at me with a face that said, *This is really bad*. There was pity in his eyes, and I find pity difficult. It was the first time I thought, 'I think he's going to die.'"

Tom needed to be seen at a large hospital. The doctor asked, "Do you want me to take him in an ambulance?" Amelia chose to drive him. "In the car, I thought to myself, 'I will remember this drive forever.' When we got there, there was a vending machine with sweets. I'd never let the children have sweets on a Monday, but he said, 'Can I have some sweets from the vending machine?' And I said, 'Yes, take as many as you like.' He said, 'Yes! Best day ever!'"

Amelia's husband arrived and told her to call Tom's father "now." I said, "Really, call Chris?' And he said, 'Yeah, call Chris now.' So I rang Chris, he rushed over, and then we all went from the front of the hospital, the bustling normal parts of the hospital, and suddenly we were in whiter and whiter, cleaner and emptier, echoey rooms. They were places I've never been to before in that hospital. In a little white cubicle, there was a terrifying doctor looking at Tom and Chris and me, and saying that he needed to be transferred to Addenbrooke's, which is a larger, more specialized hospital in Cambridge. We were taken by an ambulance to Addenbrooke's the next day. Tom loved the ambulance, he was chatting with the driver. They've got on the blue light, he loved cars and transport, he just loved all that sort of stuff.

"At the pediatric oncology day centre, a whole group of doctors was huddled over a small screen. They were looking and pointing out bits to Chris and me and saying, 'He's got a very, very large tumor in his abdomen.' Chris and I stayed calm for Tom, but I remember going to the garage to get Tom some magazaines out of my car, and getting into the driver's seat and just sitting there, screaming and crying. Then Tom had a biopsy."

At first, Tom was diagnosed with rhabdomyosarcoma, which has a cure rate of 70 percent. "I was thinking, 'Oh, seventy percent, it's okay.' And then we came home, and they did some more testing and the oncologist phoned up and said, 'We got the diagnosis wrong, it's something else. I want you to come in tomorrow. I'm not going to tell you what it is over the phone because you'll google it.' And I said, 'No, you have to tell me now.' And she said, 'It's DSRCT.' And as I said it, Anna, my oldest daughter, googled it on her phone and went, 'Look.' We both found out together sitting in a car at a red light, that the mortality rate is very, very high for DSRCT. That he was going to die."

Tom began his first round of intense chemotherapy. "His little body was just pumped full of poison. He used to have these bags hanging up next to the wall marked TOXIC with red letters. And horrible stuff going into him for five days at a time with no letup. All these fluids being pumped through his system and all this hair falling out. And then he had a nasogastric tube, because he wasn't eating, because he was sick all the time." His immunity plummeted and he was at risk of catching anything. "We'd have days out. We went to see the Tower of London with my sister, Sharman, and Tom's little brother, Jakey, and I knew he'd get ill. It was like pandemic time. It was the same sort of feeling of viruses everywhere. As we came back on the train, his temperature went sky-high and that meant he had to go to a hospital straightaway and have intravenous antibiotics.

"Tom hated hospital at the beginning. He hated injections. He was absolutely furious at the whole thing at the start. We all wished we were the ones who had gotten sick, and not Tom.

"When the UK doctors said they had run out of treatment options and would not operate to remove the mass because it was not responding to chemotherapy, Amelia asked, 'If he doesn't have any more treatment, what's going to happen?' They said, 'He'll die within about three months. He'll have kidney failure or heart failure.' I said, 'Well, my eldest sister, Fleur, and her husband, Len, live in America, and she found some American doctors who might be able to help.' And the oncologist said, 'Yeah, don't go there. They will charge you huge amounts of money and there's nothing they can do, and you'll be so far from home if he dies there.' We had a Skype call that evening with a surgeon and oncologist at Memorial Sloan Kettering Cancer Center. They were so nice. They said, 'Your English doctors aren't wrong, but we'll give it a go if you will. We'll operate. We're not promising anything. And nothing they've said to you in England is wrong. They're good guys.'

"In England, our oncologist continued to discourage us, but I said, 'We won't be miserable in America because my sister lives there, and we'll have a fun time.' And we did. Tom loved New York and being with his aunt and uncle. He just loved all the sites and Central Park, and he loved the delis and all the kinds of burgers and big pretzels. He loved art, he loved MoMA. He just loved the whole thing of New York.

"The operation took about eight hours. The surgeon came and told Amelia, 'It's been a good day. I got it all out.' I just kind of burst into tears and hugged him, and he went, 'No, it's Him up there.' And he pointed to God. He was very religious. He said, 'Don't thank me, thank Him.' He was a nice, nice man."

Tom recovered at his aunt and uncle's house. "He watched loads of inappropriate films. Because I thought, 'Oh, there's no point.' I let him play games like *Call of Duty* too. Now my youngest, Jakey, still says, 'You let Tom play *Call of Duty* when he was ten,' and I say, 'Yeah, but Tom was dying.' I was going to let him do what he wanted, really."

Tom continued chemotherapy back in England, and as Amelia recalls, "he grew up so quickly. His thirst for life was strong. He learned to fly and went to school whenever he could because he loved his friends. He was even in a play. He went to music festivals and managed to dance to his favorite band! He became very wise. I remember coming back from one of our chemo trips to London, and he said, 'Mum, I love sleeping, and death is just like sleeping, so I'm not afraid of death, just worried how sad you will be.' He was only thirteen."

The family made two more trips to New York. During one, "They put little monoclonal antibodies in his tummy, which were soaked in radioactive material to try and kill the cancer. In the summer of 2014, Tom had his last operation, and the surgeon and the oncologists explained that the cancer had returned, dotted all over his abdomen, liver, and chest, and there was nothing more that could be done but to let him die. The cancer would continue its journey unabated and eventually kill him within months."

Amelia remembers trying to explain this to Tom, as they sat in a McDonald's in New York. "He asked what we should tell his friends in school when we returned to the UK. I looked at his beautiful sculpted face, his straw-blond hair sprouting, and I said, 'Well, that you had another operation, but this time they could not get rid of it, so there is no more treatment.'"

Tom asked about more chemo, and then he asked how long he had. "It's hard to say; they haven't given a number," Amelia told him. "How long?" "I don't know, Tom, but we're probably not looking at years." Amelia recalls Tom's face turning ashen. "'Months?' And then he runs out of McDonald's into the dark empty New York streets. It was late. It was about nine or ten at night, and as I ran after him, I remember thinking, 'It's quite dangerous in New York at night.' And then I remember thinking, 'Kill us now,' because we really had had enough of it."

Back in England, "We still carried on doing things. Tom wanted to go on holidays, so we went to Portugal and had a holiday by the sea. The doctors thought we were mad for going, but Tom wasn't going to get another chance. The weekend before he died, we went to the Savoy Hotel and to a play with my family. That was the last time he was speaking lucidly. We came back from the play and my sister had organized for the hotel to leave a huge cake tray full of macaroons and little cakes, and Tom loved cakes and macaroons. And he went, 'Oh, look, it's amazing. Look at this, it's beautiful, but it's not as nice as Anna's.' (His sister is a good baker!) He was speaking for the first time in days. He'd been taking a lot of morphine, and he was on so many painkillers and pain patches that he didn't really talk.

"Then he closed his eyes and he said, 'When I close my eyes, I go into a different world. Do I make a noise? Do I make a noise when I'm in that different world?' And I said, 'No, you don't.' And he closed his eyes and then opened them and said, 'I just went there, Mum, just then. Did I make a noise? Is it embarrassing?' I said 'No,' and I said, 'What did you see?'

"He said, 'I was at the edge of a field and I was watching Jakey and one of my friends, and they were on my blue tractor and they were playing, and they were laughing, and I was watching from the side. I was waving at them.' And I kind of knew then, it was almost like he was looking on from death. It just felt really sad. But he wasn't sad. He was just saying, 'I was just waving at them and they waved back.'

"That night in the hotel, Tom fell over, and when we got home, he could no longer walk. He was in the downstairs room. And I still feel bad because I can't really remember the last words that I said to him when he was still awake, but I remember him crying for me in the night and I went to him and I said, 'What do you want? What do you want?' and cuddling him. I remember him saying, 'I'm struggling.' And I think those were his last words, 'I'm struggling, Mum.'

"I can't remember what I said back. I don't know if I said, 'I love you.' I was just so tired. Days passed, until his breathing pattern changed and we realized that he would die shortly. I had agreed with the community nurses that we wanted him to die at home, and we called Tom's dad, my sisters, and his stepsisters. The house was full, we had relatives sleeping all over the place on sofas, everywhere. All the lights were on. It just felt like a very buzzy house, really. And Tom was sleeping on a hospital bed, and I was snuggled up next to him. He had this massive tumor. It's like he was pregnant. And the tumor was forcing all his veins out, so you could see all his red veins like a jigsaw puzzle on his tummy. And his face was very thin. He had some hair. His hair had grown back because he'd stopped the chemo. I dozed on and off that night. I must have woken up probably around six in the morning. I just kept waking up to check that he was still breathing. I had my head right next to him to hear his breath, and I closed my eyes."

Amelia takes a quick breath and then recalls what happened next. "If you close your eyes and you try and imagine something, you have to conjure it up, you're using something in your brain. You can almost feel your brain working. But this experience wasn't like that. I closed my eyes, and it was like somebody simultaneously switched on a video just under my eyelids. I didn't ask for it to come there, I didn't expect it to be there. I certainly wasn't thinking about anything spiritual. I wasn't praying or anything. I was utterly focused on Tom's breathing, and the image was just there. My brain didn't think, 'Oh, this is weird.' Because I'm a solicitor, I'm very logical, I'm a very rational person, my brain doesn't compute that sort of stuff. My brain is all about logic. But I just watched every-thing like I was watching a film, but without questioning, 'What is this film doing in my brain?'"

What Amelia saw "was a woman walking toward what I thought was me. I didn't think she was coming toward Tom, because she just appeared. I watched her, and I thought, 'She's a beautiful young woman. She's so beautiful.' And I remember thinking, 'I must re-member this. I must remember this. I must remember that she's beautiful.' She had a pale face and a sort of slightly pointy chin; her face was like a heart. Very pronounced cheekbones. She wasn't anybody I recognized. She had long, dark hair that was like what women wore in the seventies, a Joni Mitchell or someone like that. And I always leave this bit out, because I think people will think I'm mad, but she was wearing like a gown. A proper gown in white. I think she might've been holding something in her hand.

"The main thing I remember thinking about her is, 'Gosh, she needs to get somewhere. She's urgent. She's purposeful.' And I re-member thinking, 'She's not late.' Like, I'm sometimes late for a meeting and out of breath. It was just that she had a look in her eyes that said, 'I must be there at this time.' She was walking quickly, with purpose and with intent. She appeared solemn, strong, and wise.

"Then I looked at what she was walking through, and it was a tunnel. I find it really difficult to describe that tunnel, because it was dark. But there was light shining through it. If I looked at the walls of that tunnel, it wasn't brick or cement. It was like air. But it was solid. So the only way I can compare it to something is that it would be like a cloud. A dark storm cloud looks quite solid, but you can see the sun behind the cloud trying to break through. It was like that white kind of winter sunshine trying to break through, and when it does, you know the sun's out. And that's what it felt like.

"Now that I've read so many books on death, I know everyone talks about tunnels. But I hadn't read those books then. I was just reading normal books. And I remember seeing the tunnel, and out of the corner of my eye, I could almost see this incredibly intense white light. And I knew that white light was really good. I knew everything was okay, because of this intense white light. The beautiful woman was just coming closer and closer to us. And then I think I opened my eyes, and it all just disappeared.

"All I thought in that moment was, 'Is Tom still alive?' What was I doing closing my eyes? He was still breathing. I just remember the last moments then of him breathing very, very gently. My heart was like, There's another breath. There's another breath. And then suddenly there was this tiny little gurgle, and then there was just no breath.

"And that's death. It's the weirdest thing to me, that that is death. I still can't get my head around it. But that is death. It seems so strange, you just don't take that breath. And that's it. And your body's still there. He was still warm.

"He was still all there to me at that moment. I could not move; I just held him. And I did feel the air was thick with a sort of anticipation. The air just felt elastic and different, and I could not move. I felt completely calm. At that moment, my sister, Sharman, opened the door. She and Tom always joked that they were 'soul mates.' She told me later that she felt like she had just entered a theater, and Tom was about to say the lines he had in a play, and I was signaling to her not to interrupt and was alive with anticipation.

"She saw Tom sitting up, with pink cheeks, his hair strong and fair, looking absolutely radiant, and he was staring with his piercing blue eyes just beyond where she was standing, like an arrow ready to fly."

Sharman, who was trained as a psychologist, described the experience, saying, "I took it as normal and had no reaction in the moment, but looking back on it now, I know it is not normal. I experienced cognitive dissonance between seeing Tom sitting up and knowing he was lying down, dead. Tom looked healthy, thick-haired and bright-eyed, staring into the distance with absolute direct purpose, as if he was about to go on an adventure."

Similar to Liz H.'s and Michelle J.'s experiences with the loss of their children, which were shared in the early chapters of this book, Amelia has also been conscious of what she believes to be Tom's presence after he died. Amelia recalls sitting with her husband on their household sofa the night before Tom's funeral. Suddenly, from out of the blue, he said, "Stop kicking the sofa, Amelia. Why do you keep kicking the sofa?" Amelia was confused and a bit shocked. "I said, 'I'm not.' And he went, 'You've just done it again. Why do you keep kicking the sofa?' And I replied again, 'I haven't.' I couldn't feel it. I couldn't feel anything. And he said, 'You keep kicking it.

Just under me. You're kicking the sofa.'" These kicks occurred "just when Izzy was saying, 'I should have done more for Tom. I should have done this. I should have done that.'" Amelia adds, "Even my husband, who is a cynic, says the timing was really odd."

The night after the funeral, Amelia recalls getting up from bed to get a glass of water. "As I was pouring myself a glass of water, the ceiling lights in the kitchen went on and off. On and off. Slowly. Not like a flicker. They'd never done it before. They started to do it a lot for the next few months, until my husband got really sick of it. He got an electrician in. And the electrician said there's nothing wrong with them. But it happened when my niece was there as well. Just on and off.

"Eventually, I did go and see a psychic, who doesn't live anywhere close to here. And she said, 'Your son's died.' In the middle of what she was saying, she said, 'He keeps playing with the lights, and he's telling you it's only to say he's around. You don't have to be worried.'"

Amelia had one other strong experience with Tom, more than three years after he died. She describes it as "an incredibly vivid dream. And I'm sure that was Tom coming to me." In her dream, she was in a garden, similar to one in the house where she grew up and where Tom loved to go. "I was putting the rubbish out, and I saw this young lad/man on the top of a hill with his back to me, and he was wearing this blue jacket that Tom always wore. And I thought, 'It's Tom.' And then this voice said to me, 'Don't be ridiculous. Tom's dead.' And then I said, 'No, that's Tom. That's Tom up that hill.' And he said, 'No, it can't be Tom.' And then I thought, 'I'm going to go and check, because what have I got to lose?'

"I remember in that dream thinking like I did with the lady in the tunnel, 'I have to remember this. This is so important.' So it was almost like there were three eyes on the dream. There was the me doing it, then there was the me saying, 'It's rubbish.' And then there was the other me saying, 'Remember this. This is so important.' And I just ran up the hill. I'm not very fit, and I remember being a bit out of breath. The lad didn't turn around, and so I just sort of put my arms around his back and thought, 'If it's not Tom, this is going to be really embarrassing, but what the hell? And if it is, I need to hold him.' Because that's what I miss. A hug. So I just put my arms around him, and he didn't dissolve into nothing. And he turned around, and he was Tom. And he was an older Tom. He was about seventeen, which is about the age he would have been when I had the dream. He was taller than me and his eyes were still blue. But one of them was paler than the other. There was a sort of paler white in the center of it. And the other one was blue.

"He just puts his arms around me. And I remember thinking, 'I've got to say something.' And I just said, 'Are you okay?' I just remember looking up at his face, and he looked down at me and he said, 'Are *you* okay?' It was like he was saying to me, 'You don't need to worry about me. It's you. What are you doing?' Because I was slammed, sad and not going out much, and moping around. And he was not like that. He didn't mope around. He sort of got on with life."

Amelia says that she "did not have any information at that time about shared death experiences," but has since read "extensively" and believes that what she experienced was an SDE. Her sister, Sharman, who came into the room as Tom died, is equally certain: "No one will convince me that these experiences did not occur, or that they were merely hallucinations." Amelia said that she'd considered sharing her experiences at Tom's funeral with her family and friends, but decided against it, worried that other people would misunderstand what she was saying and because she did not want to have to defend herself or defend her truth of what had happened.

Reflecting on the ways that her SDE has changed her, Amelia notes, "I can't do chitchat anymore." She also believes very firmly that "Tom's soul is going on. I now completely believe that we are all a soul of consciousness, which is eternal, and this soul is on this earth for a reason, encased in our mortal bodies. I believe our soul is part of a deep eternal love that is all-knowing and all-loving, and where we all come from and where we will return." And this understanding has, as it has done for other shared death experiencers, "helped my grief."

In ways comparable to Leslie and Sarah's, Amelia and Sharman's shared deathbed moments have created for each person an additional certainty about the experience. While there were differences in what they perceived, the overall effect has been to convince each of the "veracity," as Amelia puts it, or the truth of the experience. Common to many of our experiencers as well is the reluctance to speak of what happened outside their own tight circle.

There is an another significant component in Amelia's account, which is similarly mentioned by Ida N., recounting the death of her mother, and in a nongender form by Stephanie L.: the appearance of the beautiful, unnamed woman who seems in a hurry and very intent on her job. This guide to the afterlife appears frequently enough that we have identified its presence with a name: The Conductor. (The Conductor's prevalence and role will be discussed further in chapter 13.) Although not all experiencers report the presence of a Conductor, it occurs with enough frequency that I am led to ask whether this presence is a central part of conveying the departed out of this physical world.

Thus far, we have explored a very wide range of SDE moments and phenomena. Yet for all their exceptional range, these experiences share many common elements: producing a deep calm around death; being conveyed through a strong, overwhelming experience of physical sensations or a visual experience of seeing a loved one depart; or remotely receiving some type of visual or physical message from them around the time of death. For all the differences in stories and circumstances, as a researcher, I cannot help but be drawn back to the patterns and common elements across these stories, as well as their profound impact on the experiencer's grief.

We will now explore two additional stories, that of Alice W., whose husband faced a terminal cancer diagnosis, and Karen K., who married her husband knowing he had a terminal disease. These cases ask us to consider how we can prepare for death during life and what impact that knowledge has on the SDE. After exploring these stories, we will then turn to a deeper discussion of what the SDE means, why there has been resistance in some quarters to the existence of the SDE, and how SDEs can lead us to rethink our entire approach to life, death, and grieving.

11

PREPARING FOR
DEATH IN LIFE

MARRIAGE VOWS frequently repeat some variation of the line "Till Death Do Us Part," but that ending is rarely at the forefront of a newlywed couple's thoughts, if at all. That was certainly the case for Alice W., who was born in Atlanta and moved to France to study and then stayed to work. "I met my husband at this very ritzy place called the Racing Club in Paris, where neither of us ever went, before or after. It was a total coincidence. There were some expats there, and it was a big evening. I came very late because my taxi got lost. I arrived almost at dessert time, and at my assigned table, there was no more room. Someone at the next table said, 'Oh, come sit with us.' And that's how we met."

Gert was forty, Alice was forty-four. "I'm a very passionate person, a literature professor and a writer, and he's the guy who was levelheaded. He worked at a bank in Austria until he moved to a job in international diplomacy. We were just total opposites, but very complementary at the same time. He kind of kept my feet on the ground in many ways. He's a rock you can lean on."

Alice laughs and adds, "He didn't tell me in our marriage contract that it was written in fine print, *You have to know how to ski*. Growing up in the American South, I had not skied. I wanted to ski the easiest slopes, and he put me on the hard slopes. His trick was to try and get me to sit down in his lap and slide down that way. Apparently, it had worked to charm other women in the past. But I was so mad that I skied down that slope. So that was our relationship: sporty, intellectual.

"I was mad at him a lot, because he didn't have enough time for me. He was passionate about his work. I called him Napoleon because he slept five or four hours a night, which was not good for his health, that's for sure. And then the ultimate trick he played on me was to leave me here on earth all alone. So I wish I hadn't complained so much about him working all the time."

Alice explains, "I was sick with migraines, with exhaustion from my commute. I feel like I should have died. I was the one who was fragile and not my husband. He never got sick. And then he gets this diagnosis of stage-four prostate cancer. He was fifty-two, and I almost had a nervous breakdown, but that's my personality. I just get really upset; I started using 'we,' all the time as if we were both ill. I wanted him to know we were a team." Gert did not want to undergo surgery or chemotherapy. Instead, he opted for hormone therapy. "His decision was not to do anything invasive. He lived very well on hormonal therapy, or as well as you can, for three years.

"And how did he handle his illness? He was probably the best patient a doctor could hope for. He worked for an international organization as a macroeconomist. And so he was extremely well organized. He had duplicates of everything. Everything was documented. When he went to the doctor's office, he had more information than the doctor did. He filled in all the missing blanks. He never complained. And maybe that's one reason I just couldn't believe he was going to die. He had a smile on his face till the end. Everybody adored him. He was just a gentle person. A really easygoing guy, sort of Buddha material. Nonconfrontational."

But Gert did not modify his behavior. It was as if he did not want to acknowledge the disease. Alice recalls, "I was stupefied by the fact that he didn't change his lifestyle in the way I thought he should have, in terms of eating and things like that. And he started going back to working himself to death. In the end, he wished he hadn't. When we got to the fourth year, the signs started looking really bad, and the doctors didn't have solutions for my husband. We were like a ship on an ocean in May, June, July, August, the last four months, in and out of the hospital. They will be forever branded in my heart as a tragedy. At this stage, the cancer had devoured my husband's body. His legs were paralyzed. He told me that he didn't want to live, if that continued. He had so much morphine that it kept him from being in much pain. The main thing was to keep him out of pain. I did reflexology also, and it somehow worked on him. I could not accept the fact that he was going to die." She adds, "Even when it was perfectly obvious, I told him that there would be a miracle. I was sure there would be a miracle."

Alice was constantly in the hospital. When she left to go home to sleep, "my name was written as big as a poster, 'Madame W.,' with my telephone number. Everybody knew me, and I said, 'Please call me anytime. Anytime, I'll be there.'" On the night of August

26, Alice recalls that she slept quite well. "But I always had my telephone. It's an iPhone. It's always on. I always double-check. It was
on that night. At nine o'clock the next morning, I'm about to get
into the elevator. And I get a telephone call from the doctor who
runs the hospice, who tells me that my husband passed away between three and six in the morning.

"And I said, 'How is that possible? You promised to call me.'
He told me, 'We did call you, the nurses called you, everyone tried
to call you.' I raced over and I went into my husband's room. It
was beautiful, with a candle and some flowers. And it was quiet. I
looked at his face, and he looked almost as if he were smiling. He
had a beautiful smile of perfect peace. I asked to speak to nurses, to
try to learn why they didn't call me, because I had no trace of any
calls on my phone. I got an appointment for a week later.

"A week later, I realized that I had had this experience, which
took place when I was asleep in bed. But first, I'm going to tell you
about the interview I had with his nurse. I said, 'Why didn't you
call me?' She answered, 'I did call you a half a dozen times. I don't
understand why you didn't answer. I even tried to call other people
and they answered, but your phone didn't answer.' And I said, 'Well,
that's impossible because I'm a very light sleeper. And especially in
this situation. I don't sleep through any phone calls.' I put her on the
spot, but now I believe she was telling the truth. She had no reason
not to." Instead, Alice concluded that the calls from the nurses never
reached her.

"And now I'm going to tell you the reason why I didn't answer
the phone: because my soul had left my body. My soul was with my
husband, and I am absolutely convinced of it. I have no scientific
proof, but for me, it's perfectly obvious. I found myself behind my

husband, who is going up into the blue sky. And there's this feeling of perfect beatitude. It was perfect, perfect peace, kind of what I saw on his face when I walked into his room that morning. In this experience, I couldn't see his face exactly. It wasn't as if I could see my husband physically, but I was following him into the heavenly spheres, into blue light and white clouds. I don't know how high I was, but I was up there with him, and I kept following him and following him. And at one point, I made the decision to come back. I'm sure I didn't actually have the choice; I think I had to come back. If I didn't, I would have to die. So I had the consciousness that if I continued to go with him, then that would be my end. There was no fear, I just said, 'I don't think I can go any farther for the moment.' Then I turned around, and it was as if I could see the earth from hundreds of thousands of kilometers from where I was. If you've ever studied the Old Masters, Hieronymus Bosch, or Breughel in the Renaissance, they drew all kinds of weird things, horrible things on earth. I turned around, and I see the earth the way I've never seen the earth in my entire life. I saw all this treason and treachery; it was almost like I was looking at hell, although I didn't think that at the time."

Alice describes the entire experience as not having any physical component. "We were in the house of the soul. 'Myself' didn't really exist. There were parallels between the feeling that one might feel if you're in a trance, coming out of your body or not feeling the chair beneath you anymore, things like that. But this is an even more powerful feeling—it was absolute, perfect bliss, something I had never felt before and have never felt again. I was there with my husband, my beloved husband, who was no longer ill and was about to move into another sphere."

She adds, "I can't prove it. I don't want to prove it. But the time frame corresponds to when I was asleep. Many of these questions that are scientific are going to be impossible to answer because what happened to me is not scientific. For me, it was obvious that it was my husband. He passed away in that time period, and I was with him. He didn't give me his ID and say, 'Bring this back home,' or he didn't cut off a lock of his hair, and I didn't wake up with it in my hand, there's no empirical evidence. I can't even tell you if it lasted a half second or three hours; I wouldn't even know."

In the beginning, Alice says, "I would tell people about it, but I think they just thought I was totally nuts, to be perfectly honest. I didn't realize it initially, and then I just stopped talking about it." The only one who was receptive was Alice's priest, who had married Alice and Gert and also celebrated Gert's funeral mass. "For him, it was quite natural. And he explained it. He said, 'Of course, it's normal.'"

But despite the many people who rejected her story, Alice nevertheless describes the aftermath of her SDE as being truly life altering. "I don't know whether my change in the way I see the world . . . how much of that is due to losing my husband, mourning, and how much is due to this shared death experience, but something has changed so absolutely radically inside of me. The only thing I want to do is try to be a better person, finish doing what I need to do, do things the right way, the way my husband would want me to do them, and try and help other people. And the day that the good Lord wants to take me, I will be so relieved.

"I think my husband's in Heaven. I think I went to Heaven with my husband and then returned to Earth. And I do believe in Heaven. I wouldn't have said that before. My husband was Catholic, and it's made me integrate into the Catholic Church, but I'm also very skeptical. I come from a very intellectual family, we started out as Lutheran, my father converted to Judaism, and my mother had a doctorate in philosophy and said she was a 'pantheist,' which doesn't mean I can't be religious, but I think we all have our own way of expressing what is spiritual. Some people use religious terms. It's possible for me to do so, but to be perfectly honest, I'm more and more convinced that we can't explain these things. And if we could, we'd be God, or whatever you want to call whatever is overseeing us."

Like Alice, Karen K. believed her husband was never going to die. When they met, the first thing she noticed about Timothy was his voice. He was a musician by training, and he had "this astonishingly pure voice." They had both grown up in towns along Australia's east coast, had both been active in youth groups, had both chosen teaching as their profession, and shared many of the same memories and values. She recalls, "He was a painter and a musician, so a very creative individual. And he was very Irish in his ways, not that he was born in Ireland, but his Irish ancestry lent itself to a very polite, welcoming, warm household, and that's a lot of my background as well."

Timothy was twenty-four and Karen was twenty-two when they started dating. "I kept popping around to visit, and he kept calling me and putting letters in my letter box. We started going out and a couple of weeks into our relationship, he said he had 'something to tell' me. He told me that he was born with a terminal illness. He was completely well at the time, and he said, 'Oh, look, it would probably take a Mack truck to knock me over.' And in many ways, it did. It was an interesting journey. There were many times where he was absolutely emaciated and ill, but yet we would be laughing about the state of the world."

In the beginning, however, there was no inkling for either Karen or Timothy of what was to come. "When I met him, he was really doing so much. I remember thinking, 'How can I be with this person? He's too busy. He's got too many projects going on.' I didn't know whether I could cope with that level of intensity. But then things slowed down when illness crept in. So things had to change. It turned our world on its head, really.

"I was with him for fifteen years, and he had a double lung transplant during that time. Many people who get a double lung transplant live for about five years; Timothy lived for ten. Our experiences took us to the depths of what illness and facing death on a daily basis can do. When you choose to be with someone who you know is going to die, but quite intellectually you can't really hang on to that concept . . . but at the same time, in your heart, you know it, it's a really challenging position to be in. I chose to stay with my husband and love my husband. If you had met him, you would have loved him too."

Karen describes her husband as someone who "never wanted to put anyone out." She recalls that they received the call for his transplant surgery on a Sunday, making the journey to the hospital miles away in Sydney easier. "With a lung disease, even getting him from the bed to standing position, that's very difficult when someone's actually suffocating. And then getting him into the car with oxygen attached." When they arrived, they were "greeted by a woman with blond curly hair who was so excited to see us. To me, that's a spiritual experience, to meet someone on the way who could give us that energy and positivity at that time.

"Timothy's most used words were 'thank you,'" Karen notes. When he awoke in intensive care after the surgery, "His eyes were still closed and he could not speak, but he took my hand and with his finger wrote *thank you* into my palm over and over again and pointed toward the nurses and doctors that stood working beside his hospital bed." After the surgery, the couple picked up the pieces of their life, Timothy continued to write music and lyrics, and they had a child. Three months after their daughter was born, he was diagnosed with cancer, a possible consequence of the many immune-suppressing drugs he needed to take to prevent him from rejecting his new lungs.

What followed were months of hospitalizations and surgeries. "The level of suffering that he endured was really quite astronomical and devastating," Karen says. "I think he gave absolutely everything he could to our family, even though it was difficult at times to give anything at all because of the illness.

"Before he had the lung transplant, he had been declining in breath, but it was a really slow decline over many years. This was a faster decline. Within one year, it was a devastating loss. Even moving him to lie down in the bed could take up to forty-five minutes. He ended up in a wheelchair because he couldn't breathe, and we had oxygen going on at the house all the time." Karen found herself trying to divide her energies between Timothy and their daughter. "The suffering for all of us was very difficult," she says, but yet "I didn't really believe that he was dying, even in the last days. He did say that his brother was with him—his brother had died quite a long time ago. He said he could see a tunnel, but he didn't want to go down the tunnel. And he did talk about his brother, who was saying to him that everything was going to be okay."

Karen and Timothy returned to the hospital, and Karen says, "I was still thinking that a miracle would come and that he would be okay, because we'd had a miracle before. We'd had the lung transplant. That was a miracle, so I was expecting another one. We had lots of people praying for a miracle, and we were trying every last thing to save Timothy's life.

"At nine o'clock each night, there were many people in their homes praying or singing for Timothy. On this particular night, a Saturday, his mother, his sister, and I were there in the hospital room with him. He kept winking at me and said, 'That's my beautiful wife,' and he told us that he loved us. When nine came, we all closed our eyes to pray, and Timothy closed his. I believe that was when he went into a coma. He looked asleep; his mom and sister were just happy that he looked so peaceful.

"During the night, I saw that his breathing didn't seem right." The doctor told Karen that Timothy was unconscious, and the end was coming. "He said that Timothy could hear everything, but just not respond. From that moment until late that night I didn't stop talking to him. I spoke to Timothy about how much I loved him and that our daughter and I would be okay, and I would ensure that our daughter would know her father, and how he was my love. I also promised I would go back and visit places that he loved.

"With the immunosuppressant drugs, you have to worry about the sun all the time, but that afternoon, at one point the sun was shining on his face through the window, and I said that he didn't need to worry about the sun anymore. He didn't have to worry about any more tests or swabs or medicine or oxygen. There was no more waiting for results.

"For the first time, my daughter and I could actually go up close to him, and cuddle and kiss him, which is not possible when you have someone suffocating with lung disease. When you have no breath, you can't have anyone close to you because they will take your air and it's too much of a struggle.

"We also bathed Timothy. He always liked to feel clean and respectable, so we did that. I even washed his feet, which in the Catholic tradition was very meaningful for me. His sister and mother were there when we did that, which was a massive thing, because Timothy's brother had died in a work accident. They didn't get to say goodbye to him. But they got to say goodbye to Timothy.

"While he was in the coma, I said to him that I wanted him to open his eyes one last time so I knew he could hear me. Unbelievably, over the following hours, he began to open his eyes as I talked. He even tried to talk back, but he couldn't talk at that point." But Karen says, "I knew he'd come back to see me.

"I closed the door, and I knew I had to stay with him until his last breath. I pulled the chair up to the bed and took his hand. I said that it was quarter past two in the morning, and that there was no one else there, that it was just me, and that I would not leave him, and that I was right here, and that I was carrying him. I told him how much I loved him, and that he was my life's revelation. One of his songs was called 'Revelation.' I said that our daughter would be okay, and that we were okay right now, and that my mother and father had our daughter, and that they were taking care of her. I sang some of the first lines of his song to him.

"I sang other songs too, and his breath changed. Three breaths, not regular, but the raspy kind, until he breathed his last breath. I said aloud, 'It is done.' I don't know where those words came from, but they weren't mine. His spirit left his body, his whole being went and stood behind my right shoulder. It was almost like this side of my head was completely activated. It was like I had a different vision coming through from my right side. It was like a movie camera in my head giving me a different way of seeing. In that vision, I saw Timothy's whole self. He was alive, moving, cartwheeling, somersaulting, running, and whooping down the hospital hallway—not in the room I was standing in, but the hallway. I could see him going up and down. He was totally exuberant.

"He was younger, he was as young as when I first met him. He looked brilliant. His energy was absolutely boundless, and he was happy and free. He came right up to my face and showed me his face, and his happiness. Then the hospital wall, it's hard to describe, it's like it disappeared.

"There should have been a room right next to us, but instead we were at the edge of the building. Out there, even though it was just after two in the morning, was a pink sky, and then sort of gray clouds that come through the pink and orangy colors. It was almost like dawn. For me, it was beautiful to see that. I then saw Timothy's body as a heat haze, changing and melding into that view, and it drifted out, into that pink sky. It just melted into the sky. I could see it moving out and beyond.

"He didn't say the words, but the understanding was that he was going home. For me at that moment, he was going to our home to see our daughter. The following day when I spoke to my mother, she said that around that time my daughter actually awoke and needed to be resettled. For me, I absolutely knew he'd gone to see her.

"After he went out into that sky, I was in awe. I was so happy because he was free. After seeing so much suffering, he needed to show me that he was exuberant and light-filled. I rang the nurses' buzzer and was so ecstatic and excited. The nurse came in, and I said how happy I was because I was there for his last breath, just like he wanted me to be."

Karen continued to feel Timothy's presence, both in the days immediately following his death and also at other times that were more removed. "My father came to get me from the hospital. I was sitting in the car, and on the way home, I felt that Timothy was with me in the car . . . like a ball of energy is how I'd describe it. He was trying to make me laugh, and I was saying things like 'I'm in the car with my father, and you're dead, so stop making me laugh.' The following day I remember I was in the bedroom, and he was actually moving around me, being cheeky, like he always was, being absolutely cheeky and poking me to make me laugh. I actually said to him, 'You're dead. I'm supposed to be upset. What am I going to do with you?' It was a joyful experience."

But this was not to be Karen's only experience with death that year. "A week after Timothy died, my father was diagnosed with terminal cancer, and he died six months later. His brother—my godfather—was also diagnosed with cancer, and he died shortly after my father. Several months passed, and my grandfather died. Because of Dad's terminal illness, my mother couldn't be there to support me; she needed to focus her attention on my father's health. I was left alone with my daughter, and for the first time, I felt largely abandoned—not by anyone's fault, but that's just the way things were. What the SDE helped me with was . . . it enabled me to tell my father and my godfather about what had happened. I don't exactly know what it did for them, but I felt such a need to tell them. Recently, I talked to a friend of mine whose son had died in an accident a year before my husband died. I told her about my SDE experience. It was such relief for her. She described how she saw the mist of her little boy. It's really important to share this experience with the right people at the right time.

"The grief has been really devastating, but I find that Timothy is with me when I'm most joyful. Sometimes, I will go to touch my daughter in a certain way or wink at her, or do something, and I actually think, 'Oh no, that's Timothy doing that' or even 'That's my father doing that.' I actually just know immediately. It's a knowing that they are with me, part of me, an inherent knowing without explanation. That's how it feels to me."

Karen says that her SDE is part of the overall love story she shared with Timothy. "I feel like this is my work in some ways to present you with a love story, what death, dying, and bereavement mean for people, but what it means for afterlife as well. Do we talk about death and dying? No, we don't. How do we treat bereaved people? In the Western context we're not good at it. We isolate bereaved people, and they're largely silenced and marginalized.

"Two weeks before Timothy's death, I formed the belief that we are just dead in the ground, because I couldn't hold any belief at that point. But now I don't fear the death transition at all because, well, why should I? I saw something beautiful and fantastic and life-giving, not life-taking. Even if it lasted only for a second, or if it lasts for Timothy's spirit life forever, he got to receive that, and to me, that has changed my mind about people going.

"I kept looking for a medical miracle, for two new lungs, anything. I didn't realize, but the miracle was actually in his dying and me seeing the SDE. That was the actual miracle."

·   ·   ·

We have come full circle, harkening back to the experiences of Gail O. and Michelle J. from the start of this book. Gail felt transported outside of her father's hospital room, which is similar to how Karen felt transported out of the room, and Michelle, who experienced the brilliant sky after her daughter's passing, much as Karen did. Here, we have three people who never met, people who did not expect to have an SDE, who had no language or frame of reference for such an event, and yet, in an instant, had their lives transformed. They have not only undergone a profound experience with their loved one, but their personal grief and their insights into death and dying have been changed.

As I began to explore more and more of these cases over the years, to hear the stories, and to see the patterns in the experiences and hear experiencers, in their own words, completely unprompted, relay the depth of the import and impact, I knew that, as Karen so eloquently puts it, I could no longer allow the bereaved to be "isolated, silenced, and marginalized." The SDE had to come out in the open and become part of our cultural understanding of death and loss.

But this raises another fascinating set of questions: We know that there are SDEs. You have just read powerful and diverse accounts on these pages. They have a name. Then why, given the SDE's depth of impact, has it not been studied more? Why has it not been talked about, acknowledged, and accepted? Why do many experiencers, like Alice, come to feel an often overwhelming need to keep it to themselves? And when will that change?

These are the issues we will explore next.

12

ENDING THE SILENCE
AROUND THE SHARED
DEATH EXPERIENCE

SHARED DEATH Experiencers in their own words:

"In the beginning, I used to say, 'Do you believe me?'"

Her next thoughts were, "No one would believe me, and I wasn't sure I believed it."

"I realized how hard this was going to be to tell anyone. It transcended words."

"My husband, we've been together for twenty-five years . . . but he totally dismissed what I said. This is something I have to keep to myself."

Even sharing "a little snippet" with her children prompted a reaction where "they all looked at me, and reacted as if Mom can't handle this, Mom's gone crazy."

"I would tell people about it, but I think they just thought I was totally nuts, to be perfectly honest."

• • •

In this book, you have heard from a wide range of people, young, old, some with advanced degrees, many with lengthy careers. Some are parents; others are educators. Some have worked for the government; others have been part of large companies. Some work in health care. A significant number have scientific or technical backgrounds. Many also describe themselves as skeptical by nature. But they share one thing in common: they have discussed, without reservation, their profoundly transformative experiences involving the death of a loved one or a friend. Very often, they have found complete strangers to be more open to listening to them than their own families and friends.

Take a moment and ponder this: they have had what is perhaps the most profound experience of a lifetime, and the majority of these experiencers feel overwhelmingly that they cannot share it. They receive a message of disbelief—or worse. I have lost count of how many times I have heard someone say to me, "Thank you for listening to my story," or "Thank you for believing me." Let us start by trying to understand this culture of disbelief surrounding SDEs. It starts, in part, with understanding and acknowledging that as a culture, we are profoundly uncomfortable around death. More even than religion, sex, and politics, death may be the ultimate taboo conversation topic. Why that is partly has to do with the advances in modern medicine, but it also partly has to do with us.

As Dr. Monica Williams, the medical director for the Shared Crossing Project, notes, for many years, the medical education system "overselected" students for their scientific mind-set. Many of the medical professionals practicing today have been trained primarily as "body engineers." They are meant to work inside a disease-based system—that is, when they are confronted with a disease, their focus is on how to hold it at bay. No wonder, then, that medicine has become specialized: Many doctors are experts in systems or even individual organs; they treat only the region they are trained in, not the person as a whole. The advances in technologies and treatments have led patients to become the sum of their component parts.

When physicians are confronted with major or terminal disease, the central questions they ask usually revolve around trying to postpone death. Working with this model, death is equated with failure. In fields such as cancer treatment, the constant analogy is of a battlefield and going to war against the disease. The medical community rarely starts off by asking how shall we live? What are the goals for your life now? A few notable exceptions to this approach are nurses, whose training includes not simply the biological patient, but also the psychological and spiritual aspects of the patient, and also palliative care and hospice physicians.

Overwhelmingly, however, there is a lack of candid, nonjudgmental discussion around death. Even the terminology used to describe some of the events experienced around the end-of-life transition has highly negative connotations. Medical providers speak of "terminal hallucinations" to describe patients who report seeing or being aware of departed family members or friends. Medical explanations for transition moments range from "hypoxic"—meaning that they result from a lack of oxygen—to "metabolic derangement" and confusion. (Notably, many of the same explanations are also given to patients who report near-death experiences.)

If the conversation starts with the concept that the dying person is "metabolically deranged" or that what they are seeing is simply a hallucination, it is a challenge just to get to neutral, let alone positive acceptance. The medical response has often been to heavily medicate the dying, thus diminishing their experience of visions or other predeath or dying-moment experiences. Indeed, medical professionals who have encountered shared death experiences or have even been experiencers themselves are deeply reluctant to speak about them; as one put it to me, "The only people who might be able to discuss this are those whose careers are at an end. Otherwise, it is professional suicide."

But there is a similar reticence to talk about end-of-life experiences among another key player in end-of-life treatment: the clergy. Recall Stephanie's rabbi, who essentially shut down their conversation around her shared death experience with her husband. Other experiencers have not even felt comfortable enough to raise the topic with a priest or a minister. As Scott T. described it, "I felt alone for a long time . . . it felt like something I couldn't bring back to my family and my Presbyterian community. It didn't feel safe. Not that they are dangerous people or whatever, but it's just that there's a preciousness about the experience that you don't want anybody else to step on. And you don't know where people are going to come from. And so that risk of disclosure was really present for me." Very few clergymen respond as Liz H.'s minister did. He validated what she had experienced by telling her in no uncertain terms that she had been to Heaven with her son, Nicolas. Alice W.'s French priest did much the same when he declared her experience to be "normal."

This automatic skepticism or discomfort is particularly ironic given the role religion and religious communities have historically played in the transition from life to death, dating back centuries. One of the most fascinating religious artifacts comes from late medieval France, and is a text titled *Ars Moriendi* or *Art of Dying*. It has been found in various monasteries primarily in central France, a natural crossroads in Europe, often translated from the Latin. It contains specific instructions on how to care for the dying: prayers, music from the chapel, remedies for pain, bodily care, and ways to manage mental and emotional distress. *Ars Moriendi* is in many ways the Catholic monastic tradition's version of *The Tibetan Book of the Dead*, and it is surprisingly ecumenical for its time, containing guidance from Celtic, Jewish, and Islamic traditions. In other words, religious traditions shared the awareness that they needed to understand and openly minister to the dying and the soon to be bereaved. Perhaps some semblance of this view persisted with Alice W.'s priest.

Being open to the mystery of the SDE would thus seem to be a natural response among members of the religious community, but this has yet to happen in an organized way. I do not know if this is because a shared death experience is primarily nondenominational or if it takes the concept of afterlife out of very specific religious guideposts and beliefs. Some people have found that their SDE challenges their belief system. As another interviewee, Lisa J., explained to us, "I had the shared death experience, which absolutely shattered my belief system. I was raised Lutheran. My stepdad was a Lutheran minister. I was the youth leader in my church, and I believed everything that I was told, including that if you weren't baptized, you were going to hell. That's where I had so much angst about my husband . . . fearing that he was going to hell. And then, when I saw that he wasn't, that's what shattered everything for me." Yet other experiencers find themselves drawn to a more spiritual path after their SDE, even to a more explicit belief in God or a divine being. As Cristina C. said, after her SDE with her mom, "Before, I wasn't close to God at all. I could never feel God. I didn't know where He was. I was really into science. I'm the kind of person that I need evidence. And now I feel like I have to tell people about God because that's how real it was." Whatever the experiencer's ultimate religious beliefs, however, it is clear by now that a discussion of shared death experiences and the possibility of their existence has not been a widely accepted part of pastoral care or religious discussions around death.

What experiencers have communicated to us is that they are looking not simply for a compassionate ear, but for an affirmation that their experiences are valid and legitimate. A shared death experience speaks to the mysteries of the world, the meaning of life, and the meaning of divinity itself. People gather in spiritual communities primarily to experience the divine and to share their faith in some higher, loving force that cares about and guides them, so naturally, experiencers want to turn to their communities. But then they discover that their life-changing SDE is somehow questioned or diminished, in part because their spiritual or religious counselor is unfamiliar or uncomfortable with shared death experiences. Many also recoil from any expression of joy, yet experiencers do report feeling joyous. Stephanie L. noted that at her husband's funeral and during her subsequent grief, she felt it was "socially unacceptable" for her to feel joy and be okay with his death. Those of us who have roles as grief counselors need to make space for positive feelings that the bereaved may experience as a result of their SDEs. In turn, experiencers are asking their religious and spiritual communities to recognize and honor these experiences as normal, healthy, and as special gifts. To reach that point, however, is going to require some reassessment and open communication.

Examining these very divergent responses has led me to conclude that if we are to change our conversation, inquiry, and understanding around death, that change has to start from the outside and work its way in. This process is already occurring in parts of the hospice movement. Indeed, following a presentation on shared death experiences, I had a leader in hospice tell me, "This is the secret of hospice. These things happen all the time, but we don't talk about them." However, other countries are less reticent. In Great Britain, one poll found that 93 percent of "carers," as those who handle end-of-life care are called, wanted to hear more about these end-of-life experiences. A 2008 pamphlet titled "Nearing the End of Life: A Guide for Relatives and Friends of the Dying," written by Sue Brayne and Dr. Peter Fenwick and published in England by the University of Southampton, specifically addresses end-of-life experiences, or ELEs, by saying that unlike hallucinations, which are agitating and often involve very unpleasant physical sensations, "people who have end-of-life experiences seem to be calmed and soothed by them. They appear to help the person to let go of the physical world and overcome their fear of dying." When Dr. Fenwick discussed ELEs on British television, his in-box was flooded with more than seven hundred emails from caretakers and family who shared their own ELEs with friends and relatives, a phenomenon I have experienced myself when I have done interviews.

A second guide by the same authors, which looks exclusively at end-of-life experiences, recommends that caregivers and medical personnel "be interested and curious, rather than incredulous or dismissive" of these encounters. Dr. Fenwick shares his own recollection of a patient's end-of-life moment, writing, "He was going unconscious. When I looked at him, he was looking fixedly at something in front of him. A smile of recognition spread slowly over his face, as if he was greeting someone. Then he relaxed peacefully and died." Fenwick and Brayne also note, "The dying, and those who witness these end-of-life experiences, usually describe them with loving, reassuring words such as calming, soothing, greeting, comforting, beautiful, readying."

At the Shared Crossing Project, we have found the same responses as our British colleagues. So how do we change the conversation? It begins with books like this, where experiencers have the space to share their stories. It begins also with those in the hospice and palliative care communities who validate the experiences of friends and loved ones and advocate being open to these experiences. It begins with open communication among medical professionals and religious leaders. Dr. Monica Williams notes that her first SDE moment came in a consult room. A man had suffered cardiac arrest in a supermarket. He had been brought to the hospital but could not be revived. Dr. Williams had called his wife and asked her to come to the hospital, saying only that her husband was very ill. When she entered the private room to tell the woman that her husband had passed away, her response was, "I know. He just told me." That experience altered her understanding of death and led her to advocate for making space for family, friends, and loved ones even when death is occurring in a hospital. That might be as simple as giving them privacy in a room with a closed door and monitoring, but no invasive distractions. "This is a mystery that we don't have to understand," Dr. Williams says.

A majority of Americans, up to 80 percent, believe in a benevolent afterlife. But doctors tend to approach this differently. In their personal lives, they may believe in an afterlife, although surveys suggest the numbers who do are still lower than those of the general population. But professionally, having been trained on a scientific model, medical professionals frequently express skepticism or are very reticent to discuss these issues. I have interviewed doctors who have told me in effect, *Of course I personally believe in an afterlife, but I could never risk speaking about it in a professional setting.* Yet making adequate space for this discussion needs to become a fundamental part of our approach.

While medicine is geared toward data and empirical proof, there should also be a recognition that not every event must have an explanation or an airtight theory to justify it. We can acknowledge that people have a wide range of experiences around death, and all of them can be normal, and need not be explained by changes in metabolism or oxygen levels. We can identify what these experiences are, such as communicating with departed relatives and friends, and even pets, sensing their presence in the room, feelings of embarking on an impending journey, as well as reaching for people or objects, or an intense focus on windows and sources of light, or appearing deep in thought, as if processing new information. In fact, many of the elements of an SDE can be seen as signposts, letting caregivers and loved ones know that the transition to death is taking place. They can help guide the level of medical intervention, comfort, support, and management of pain. We can improve care and offer patients "a peaceful death" if we are more attuned to the signs of passing.

Already, some of the discussion around death is changing,

including an effort to identify the components of a more comfortable death. The Singapore-based Lien Foundation has twice commissioned a "Quality of Death Index," most recently in 2015, using five categories of data metrics: palliative and health care environment, affordability, human resources, quality of care, and community engagement. The index was prepared by the research unit of the *Economist* magazine. The United Kingdom topped the list, followed by Australia and New Zealand, plus several European nations and Taiwan. The United States was ranked ninth, with a score of 80.8, in large part due to the high cost of end-of-life care; on that metric, the United States scored eighteenth in the world. Thoughtful, compassionate care that could make for a better end of life may not be delivered if it is deemed too costly or not cost-effective enough.

A first step in changing the approach within the US system would be to recognize that from the moment a person receives a terminal diagnosis, every health care provider should be aware of and sensitive to the emotional pain and suffering that the patient and their loved ones will most likely be experiencing. Health care providers can learn to recognize and assist with the psycho-emotional burden of receiving and now living with a terminal diagnosis and offer options for psycho-emotional support for everyone in the family. As important as physical treatment is, it is equally important to acknowledge the deeper existential questions that often arise, like "What happens to me after I die?" Engagement in these questions may also help patients and family members talk openly about end-of-life treatment options and permit them to more honestly weigh seeking interventions aimed at prolonging life against ultilizing comfort measures that would allow for family members to connect and cherish their loved one's last days. We would do well to consider the dying person's beliefs about what lies ahead, and how they would like to transition to that destination. In many ways, the framework of the shared death experience gives space for that discussion to occur.

Next, as important as it is to listen without judgment to the dying, it is equally important to listen to those whom they have left behind. Rather than preemptively declaring shared death experiences as "unbelievable" at best or "crazy" at worst, it could be useful to be open to the possibility that they do occur. None of us benefit from dismissing these experiences or from placing intense pressure on the experiencer to keep this moment to themselves. For thousands of years, rituals and visual art forms and stories have depicted the passage from this earthly life to an afterlife. Around the world, civilizations have expressed deep connections to departed ancestors. Our disbelief is far more recent than these many centuries of tradition. Rather than dismiss or disbelieve the experiencers, perhaps we should be asking those who disagree, "How and why are you so sure?"

Because one thing I am certain of is the quality and the depth of these experiences. As Gail O. told me, in discussing her father's passing, "I can't remember exactly what I did last week. But I can remember every minute of that [the SDE]. It's a different kind of memory. It's totally part of your cell group or something. It's there and it's just so perfect a memory that it doesn't fade. No. It doesn't fade." We are witnessing a fundamental change, a true before and after, and a different way to understand this profound passage in human life.

But none of this can happen if we cannot first be honest with ourselves: death will happen. Maggie Callanan, a pioneering hospice nurse, puts it this way: "One out of one people will die . . . so the odds are against us." Death may not occur in the form we want or at the time of our choosing, but there are many ways to make it a better and more healing experience, not simply for the person who is passing but for those left behind. How we begin to do that is what I will explore in the next chapter.

13

WILL THE SHARED DEATH EXPERIENCE FIND ME?

WHY DO some individuals experience SDEs and others do not? After some two decades of study, I have several observations on this subject.

SDEs tend to occur to people who are in some way open to them and available. Frequently, they are available in a literal sense: They are not distracted; they make the time and create the space to participate in the experience. Recall Sonya F.'s reflection on her SDE with her friend Dennie: "Thinking back, I guess I felt like, in a weird way, I was available to help, so she nabbed me." Or in the case of Leslie C. and her niece Sarah, they had consciously chosen to leave the window open in the room with Leslie's dying father. Sometimes an SDE occurs when the experiencer has given the dying person permission to go, as with Karen and her husband, Timothy. Other times, an SDE can occur when the physical setting is welcoming. Richard K. was available to his longtime friend Pat when he went on a walk. Julie S. was sitting in a movie theater, an environment that already causes most of us to separate ourselves from the external world and suspend disbelief, when she became aware of her ex-husband's passing. Others find themselves at the bedside, or asleep, or inside moving vehicles (cars, planes), all locations and spaces that don't require any or much multitasking that might interrupt consciousness. Additionally, there are specific steps you yourself can take in order to become more open and inviting to, and aware of, the shared death experience. Some experiencers have practiced meditation, yoga, or other forms of mindfulness. Some are spiritually oriented or religious. Many whom we found or who have reached out to us are women, but in no way are men disqualified. Indeed, openness to the moment and the experience seems key, more than any fixed expectation that it will or won't happen.

There is also the fascinating question of how much the experiencer is aware of or literally sees around the moment of passing. Some are able to glimpse the larger "orchestration" behind the event. In the case of Ida N., from Norway, she recalls clearly seeing a "being of light" with her mother. Amelia B. had an even more distinct vision: she saw a beautiful young woman in a long white gown, holding something in her hand and moving in a very purposeful way during her son's final moments. Stephanie L. may also have experienced a vision of a guiding, energetic force with her husband. I have heard these descriptions of unfamiliar beings and individuals frequently enough to have given them a name. I have dubbed this figure or force "the Conductor," because it is clear that it has a defined, focused, even single-minded role in helping to conduct the dying person into the realm of the afterlife. Perhaps the Conductor has been more explicitly identified by earlier societies and is akin to the boatman Charon waiting at the River Styx.

In addition, the dying person may have some, or a significant amount of, say in whom they choose to share this moment with. Scott T. believes he was selected by his girlfriend's son, Nolan, because Nolan saw him as, or hoped for him to be, a father figure. Nolan also selected, out of all the relatives in the room, the aunt whom he was closest to and who had been most supportive of him and his mother. In some cases, the person selected is well equipped to act as a messenger. Richard's friend Pat may have selected him for his ability to deliver a message, just as Celia's mother possibly selected her in part for her ability to share their experience with her father and other family and friends. Something similar appears to have occurred with Sarah M. and her niece who overdosed; it was a way of communicating her experience. She adds, "My sense is that Leila's okay, that it was hard for her to exit. I'm sure she didn't want to leave her daughter, and I know she didn't, but I think she's okay."

Leslie C. discussed at length her different interpretations of the shared death experience with her father and speculated about why she was the one who ended up in the room with him when he passed away. "My reductionist mind says I was simply in the crosswalk when the bus went through the intersection—I just happened to be an observer of a phenomenon; I got lucky and got to see this. On the other hand, my dad really liked having an audience. Having an audience was one of the primary drivers in his life. He knew he had an audience because he knew Sarah loved him to death and would avidly watch whatever he did. He knew that I would sit there no matter what, because I wasn't leaving. There's that possibility. Then there's also the possibility that this was something that he wanted to be transmitted to me and to Sarah, knowing that I would tell the boys and the rest of the family that his message was 'Hey, I'm okay, guys.' Of those three possibilities, I'm happy for all of them to exist."

Cases like Leslie's do, however, illuminate a perplexing question: Why does an SDE occur for some individuals and not others? Indeed, I'm frequently asked, "Why do the departing visit only one or two caregivers or loved ones and not everyone?" It is my observation that only a limited number of loved ones are granted an SDE with the dying. Consider the case of Scott and his girlfriend's young son, Nolan. In a room full of relatives, only Scott and Nolan's closest aunt experienced an SDE at the moment of Nolan's passing. Moreover, in describing the event to me, Scott explicitly said that he believed he was "chosen" by Nolan. And perhaps there is the possibility that the dying also have an ability to indicate their preference for who will be their experiencer. Seen through this lens, the SDE takes on an additional component. Many experiencers express a belief that they were invited into the SDE for a specific purpose, such as honoring the relationship, mending a personal hurt, addressing unfinished business, or imparting an important truth, often about the afterlife. For example, in the cases of Adela B. and Ida N., their father and mother, respectively, acknowledged that their disbelief in the afterlife was misplaced. They conveyed that they had survived human death and were happy in another realm. Or in the cases of Leslie and Celia B., perhaps their individual parents chose them to be the recipients of SDEs because they believed both daughters would communicate what had occurred to other family members, that the story would be shared—as Leslie says above, "knowing that I would tell the boys and the rest of the family." Or perhaps there is a combination of both choice and availability that underlies the SDE, as indicated by the cases of Richard and his friend Pat, Madelyn and her friend Chayim, and Sonya and her friend Dennie. As Sonya explained to me, "I felt like, in a weird way, I was available to help, so she nabbed me." These disparate elements ultimately underscore the complexity of the SDE process. A complete understanding of the SDE—why it occurs, and to whom—remains shrouded in mystery.

But while there is tremendous power in the moment of the SDE, its true impact is measured in how the bereaved approach their grief and also how the SDE alters their views on death. Leslie C. says of her experience, "It gave me some peace that he was where he wanted to be. Instead of grieving for him, I can just grieve for my own loss. I can just be sad that my dad's not here, but I feel strongly that he's somewhere good and that he's happy, and he's taken care of, and that he's surrounded by love." Another Shared Crossing Project interviewee, Cindy C., explained: "It feels reassuring, really. Reassuring not only that my dad didn't have to make that journey by himself, but that maybe none of us do . . . I've never really been afraid of death. I mean, like I said, none of us are getting out of here alive. But that moment, to know that there really are other people that are waiting to go . . . 'Okay, come on. It's okay.' That's wonderful." Particularly striking on this point are Amelia B.'s reflections on her SDE with her son Tom: "It changes everything, doesn't it?" she says. "It just changes everything. I'm not frightened of death anymore. It's just slipping into a different room that we can't conceive of. Sometimes we glimpse it because our energy levels or whatever it is are aligned correctly." Of Tom, she adds, "I just feel his spirit goes on. It makes losing him bearable, 'cause I miss him. He's not here and it's not right. But I love him just as much, even though he's been dead now for six years; that doesn't change my love. My love is whole."

This leads us to perhaps the most profound implication of the shared death experience. Most grief therapy and bereavement counselors have long focused on the concepts of "letting go" and "moving on" from the deceased loved one. However, there is a new approach to grief, called Continuing Bonds, that sets aside these artificial time lines. Continuing Bonds recognizes that while the death of a loved one ends a human life, it does not irrevocably sever the relationship. Instead, Continuing Bonds opens the possibility for the surviving loved one to be able to craft a new relationship with the departed. Continuing Bonds is based on the idea that even though the deceased is no longer present in human form, the memory of them and the special bond they both shared will continue for the bereaved, only in an altered form, and this linkage deserves to be honored and cherished. In this conceptualization, the relationship is not frozen or severed, but rather, it evolves.

The concept of maintaining connections beyond the end of life is not new. Throughout most of recorded human history from the Bronze Age (2500 BCE) until just before the Western Enlightenment, most cultures and religious traditions believed in an afterlife, and many of these cultures explicitly held ceremonies to connect with their ancestors. To this day, in the early spring, many Chinese families make a trip to the graves of their ancestors to clean them, an event known as Tomb Sweeping Day. Traditional families may also maintain tablets or shrines to departed ancestors in their homes. Throughout Central and South America, many countries, particularly Mexico, celebrate the Day of the Dead on November 1, with parades, parties, singing and dancing, and visiting grave sites to honor and make offerings to deceased loved ones. While Continuing Bonds is a modern, specifically Westernized notion, it is one with deep roots, building upon the idea that death does not mean a final separation from those whom we have loved.

Within our personal experiences of grief, shared death experiences, as well as pre- and post-death experiences, can be used to affirm, process, and integrate healing for the bereaved in a way that is personal and meaningful. These are not my words; they are the independent conclusions of the SDE experiencers themselves. Another Shared Crossing Project interviewee, Yvonne K., told us, "I think SDEs can help people with their grieving process, to know that their loved one is not just ashes in the ground now, but their loved one's spirit lives on, and they've felt some of that love or beauty or seen that their loved one's spirit is living on after their moment of death. So it can be a huge comfort to people." Shared death experiencer Lynn D. explained her ongoing connection to her deceased husband to us, drawing on the words of SDE pioneer Raymond Moody: "Moody says, 'Your hearts will never be disconnected, you are always going to be connected to him.' That's the one thing about a shared death experience . . . is your hearts will always be joined. I mean, I'm never going to lose him. And you can't. There's no way. That was what kept me going." Elizabeth B., whose son, Morgan, died near the Mount Everest base camp, also described the ongoing sense of her departed son's presence: "His energy comes from my belly all the way up through my heart and it just doesn't allow me to be sad anymore. It fills me.

I don't know if I've ever heard of other people experiencing that. It's just a huge sense not just of peace, but of joy as well."

What the shared death experience also highlights is the concept of an alternative dwelling space for the souls or the energy of those who have left this earth. Again, this concept is borne out by the words of the SDE experiencers themselves and their individual descriptions. As Celia B., while reflecting on her experience surrounding her mother's death, explained to me, "I think it was very, very comforting. And I felt incredibly grateful. I knew she was in good hands and being cared for and supported." Leigh M., a hospice spiritual counselor, explained her conception of an afterlife space following her own SDE by saying during a Shared Crossing Project research interview, "We don't know exactly what goes on over there, but I think it's a nice neighborhood. I also believe that it's probably much bigger, there's a lot more dimension than what we experience here. I'm looking at this little teeny point of view from a little teeny world, and I actually think death, or perhaps that's really life, is kind of out there driving the whole thing."

Another conclusion that many experiencers draw is that an active, benevolent "next world" does exist and it follows this physical life on earth. Shared Crossing Project interviewee Julie N. concluded a discussion of her SDE with her father by saying, "It has had quite an impact on me because I know what my father and I experienced together, and even if it was some little quirky part of my brain just going off on its own fantasy, it's okay. For me, the meaning it had was, 'Hey, look what's out there. Look what's possible. Look what's next.'" Liz H., who experienced the death of one of her twins, Nicolas, right before birth, expands on this theme. "I think I was able to keep moving forward because I had this sense that it was better: wherever he was, whatever this place that he was going to be in, was better."

As part of their intellectual efforts to better define this next world and the process by which human energy reaches it, a few experiencers have even chosen to study philosophy, including metaphysics, which explores the nature of human reality, or physics—in part because quantum physics, the exploration of the universe's invisible particles, postulates that the tiniest parts of the universe are in fact both waves and particles, simultaneously. This duality, according to physicists, describes every object in existence, including people, as being both an energy packet (a wave), and a physical entity (a particle). The ability to travel between these two states makes rational sense to more scientifically minded SDE experiencers. As Brian S., whose wife died after an extended battle with cancer, explains in these pages, "I do have some sense that there's life here as we know it and then there's a different life after we've dropped our body and are in our energy bodies or whatever that is." Or as Laura T. told our research team, her SDE with her mother gave her "this knowing that she's just going on the next leg of her journey that I don't get to go on, but there will be some level of communication we'll get to continue."

Indeed, another key facet of the SDE Continuing Bonds approach is that it makes space for those of us still on earth to directly continue a relationship with the person who has passed. Many Continuing Bonds proponents actively support individuals who report after-death communication and continuing or evolving relationships, even though this deviates from the more traditional approaches to grief. That point is central to the many SDE experiencers who shared their stories with me for this book.

Michelle J., who lost two children and now works with Helping Parents Heal, commented, "There's not a whole lot of people in my world that will openly talk about these kinds of things. And even leaders in Helping Parents Heal . . . a lot of them don't get any signs at all. So I almost feel like if I talk too much about my experiences with my kids, I'm bragging, although I'm not bragging. I just feel like I have a particularly incredible connection." Other experiencers express feeling various levels of guilt about not having grieved in the expected ways, because they have chosen to follow a different emotional route after their SDE.

Experiencers offer some of the clearest descriptions of the process of maintaining and pursuing relationships with those whom they have lost. Adela B., both of whose parents died, describes the nature of her ongoing relationship with them: "Now my mom appears to me; other times, my dad does. I think the more I want to talk with them, the more they show up for me. They're busy, they're carrying on with their lives, whatever that means. I don't think this plane is all that significant to them. They're only kind to me because I'm still here . . . that's kind of how I see it." Scott T., who lost his girlfriend and her young son in a car crash, explains his continuing relationship, which he has maintained partly through meditation. "I've done lots of meditations in my life. And sometimes Mary Fran will come in and sometimes she won't. But Nolan has always been with me. If you think of him like a guardian angel, he's like right there. I know and feel his presence, and I can call on him at a moment's notice or have him appear when he wants to make himself known. I can sense his energetic signature, and I know it. And we've communicated a lot."

But this communication need not be verbal. Michelle, whose

newborn son died and whose teenage daughter later passed away following a car crash, described some of the means of communication she has encountered. "I sound like I'm crazy, but I know when it's a sign from her or when it's a sign from both of them. I don't often feel that it's a sign from Ben on his own. He sends me messages with electronics. He makes lights flash and does crazy things and light switches turn off by themselves, and I know it's him." Other experiencers have used the Continuing Bonds element of the SDE to actively work to repair their relationships. Trudy B., who experienced an SDE with her mother, described this process. "As difficult as my relationship was with my mother, from my own inner work and forgiveness, I have been able to now have the relationship with her that I always wanted. I feel her presence, her love, and her support and I have had this experience validated on several occasions, so I know that it is real."

A shared death experience can also prompt people to look outward and reassess their external lives. This theme is almost universal among shared death experiencers and is reflected in a variety of ways. Carl P. discussed the lingering impact of his SDE with his father by saying, "It's been a source of strength for me. It's emotional for sure, but I draw strength from knowing that he's there—wherever that is. And that it's not this end, and it's not nothing. It's all a mystery." While experiencers find that having others validate their SDE is very affirming and helpful, it is important to note that these changes occur whether or not the experiencers share their SDEs with other people, or whether or not other people believe them. Stephanie L., whose family, friends, and even clergy dismissed her experience, spoke of the changes she made and how she renewed her life after her SDE with her husband. "Everything became extreme, in a very beautiful way. I started planting a vegetable garden. I started listening to music. I was an art major, I went back to my art. All my senses just became so much more intense, so much more real than they had ever been."

There is also a deep realization that life is short and now is the time to readjust their lives, recognizing the insights revealed by their SDE. Experiencers often make significant life changes in primary relationships, lifestyle, and work. Indeed, the sustained depth of personal change following an SDE has led me to conclude that one major impact of the SDE is to awaken individuals to the deeper meaning and purpose of their lives in ways that they just had not been in touch with previously. As one client said to me, "My SDE awoke my true purpose in this life and gave me a sense of meaning that I had not been in touch with previously. After my SDE, I remember thinking, 'I need to let go of my primary relationship, change my health practices, and finally start my own consulting business.' And now three years later I have done just that, and my life is so fulfilling." Amelia B. also notes that she thought deeply about her larger purpose on earth after the death of her son Tom. "This life is very important. It's not flippant what we do and say and feel on this earth. But I don't think that when we go to wherever, they're going to say, 'Hmm, you only have fifty thousand dollars in your account and you didn't do that well in your job.' I just do not think that's what it's about. There's something more." Liz H., who also lost a son, echoes this same theme, saying, "I think that was an awakening for me that I had a bigger purpose than I had initially realized and that I needed to be awake and observant of how I could help people. And that there was pain in a lot of people's lives that we don't know, and that perhaps everything from that point on has really stacked up the way it was supposed to."

•   •   •

After thousands of hours of conversations with bereaved families, friends, and SDE experiencers, I have become very aware that we cannot predict which gifts or which awareness the SDE experience will share with us, and that is part of its impact and its mystery. As I was concluding work on this book, my father began the process of dying. He had been declining for years with Alzheimer's disease, but now his time had come. Because he was close to death, our family was allowed to be with him at the memory care facility where he resided, but because of the Covid epidemic, we could not go in and out of the room as we pleased. We had to choose to stay briefly or for hours and entering and exiting required us to don full PPE.

My father and I had not always had the easiest relationship. He was an international businessman who traveled a lot while my mother stayed home with three kids. I, in particular, was a high-energy kid and hard to manage, and I know I tested the limits of both my parents. But one incident literally and figuratively fractured my connection with my father and would serve as a defining moment in my life. At the start of this book, I described the skiing accident I had at seventeen. The accident was so physically devastating because when I fell, my ski boots did not separate from my skis. The reason for that was that my bindings were too tight. And the person who had set those bindings was my dad. My dad was the technician for all our ski equipment; I didn't know how to adjust them myself. In the worst confluence of circumstances, I was in a rush to leave for the slopes, he was overburdened with work, and neither of us changed our schedule so that he could adjust my bindings, because what was the worst that could happen? In a few seconds, we both learned the answer to that question. My fall on the slopes that day was not particularly bad, but because my skis didn't come off, I broke my back.

That moment set my life on a very different path, one that diverged from my father's definition of success. He never told me specifically what to do with my life, but he wanted me and my brother to choose rewarding careers. However, we differed on our definition of rewarding, and my dad assumed that I too would want a lucrative professional life. Yet throughout this time, I was living with chronic pain from my ski accident; walking and sitting were a challenge. Being a successful businessman and making money were of little interest to me. I was focused on healing and making sense of my life. Increasingly, I turned to spirituality, finding that Buddhist mindfulness practices helped me make peace with my physical suffering. My father, a devout Catholic, could not understand my new spiritual aspirations. While neither of us wanted this separation, our different outlooks created distance between us.

When I initially chose social work and teaching as a profession, and later studied theology and philosophy in graduate school, my father's prevailing attitude was, "When will this phase of your life pass, and you decide to go out and earn a good living?" He appreciated all my education but remained baffled about how I might use it in a practical way. After I became a psychotherapist, he was more accepting, but not really pleased. For my entire adulthood, I yearned to connect with my father in a meaningful way, a way that would make him see and appreciate me. I know he wanted this as well, but we remained like two separate islands, leaving each of us disappointed and frustrated with the other.

Now, as he lay dying, I wondered if we could make amends. Quite similar to the experience of Karen with her husband, Timothy, I was at last able to touch my dad. He wasn't a touchy-feely kind of guy, so we had never been physically close, but on this day, I put my head near his, and I could smell his scalp, the same smell I remember from when I was a small child and he would come home and pick me up. I prayed to God; I asked for angels and spirit guides. I talked to him and apologized for being a cause of suffering to him. We waited for three days, and on the fourth day, I knew that my father was going to die. My brother, who is a physician, later said that he felt the same way. We both recognized that we all, particularly my mom, needed to be present at his bedside.

At one point he stopped breathing for about forty-five seconds, and we thought he had died. But then the labored breathing started up again. I was sitting with my mother, my sister, and my father, and suddenly I felt presences in the room. The light was different. My body was vibrating, things were slowing down, and I was being drawn into this very mesmerizing place. And as I looked up, I saw my grandmother. But she wasn't seeing me. I realized that I'd broken into a scene that was already underway. Hovering directly above the foot of my father's bed, I could see my grandmother in traditional Irish attire. While I don't recall her dressing this way when I knew her, the vision made intuitive sense because she was very proud of her Irish Catholic roots. My auntie Joan was also there. But then a guy on the right got my attention, and I realized that it was my grandfather, the man I'm named for, whom I never met because he died when my father was fourteen.

All I could think was, "Oh my God, this guy's an energetic force." His face was very big and light. His eyes were big. He was dressed in a formal suit and tie. And he started moving forward to the bedside. I watched him go right up to my mother and say, "You don't know me, but I know you. You've loved my son very well." And I said out loud, "Mom, Grandpa Bill's right on you. Do you feel him?" And she replied, "What?" And I said, "Grandpa Bill is thanking you for being a good husband to Bob." She started bawling. And my sister started crying. Then all of a sudden Grandpa Bill sheepishly backed away. It was almost like he was in trouble and had done something wrong. I asked, "What just happened?" and my grandmother and auntie Joan cast their eyes and attention upward; they didn't say anything.

I moved my attention in the direction of their glance, and I sensed a dominant presence. Suddenly I realized, *Oh my God! You're the Conductor*. Electrical sensations moved through my body, producing tears of awe. I realized that this Conductor was what had told my grandfather to go back. Told him that now was not the time. I looked around and glimpsed more relatives; I could feel the presence of my father's childhood friends from Catholic school. We were all waiting for these assembled spirits to take my father. As I watched this scene, I noticed a channel of light extending from my grandparents to about a quarter of the way to my father. I shared this with my mother and sister and added, "I don't know why they aren't taking him." Then my mom called out, "They aren't taking him because I won't let him go." She was holding him tight and then, with a voice full of heartfelt release, she said to my father, "You can go! Oh, Bob, I love you! Thank you for all you have given me! Go and be with your father now!"

My attention moved back to the Conductor's hovering presence in the room. I can best describe it as a force. I clearly recognized that this force was serious, it was all business, it was doing a job. It was going to bring my father to his spiritual home. And I felt its power in the room. I tried to say, *I see you. I appreciate you. Thank you for doing this so lovingly to my father. He's ready.* I had the sense that this force was lining things up. There was a vortex or some kind of energetic place that he was preparing, and that vortex was going to draw out my father's soul. I had the sense that everyone assembled was saying, "We're here to greet. We've been given our instructions. We don't know when, but we're waiting, we're here."

My father's breathing became more labored. My brother arrived, and my sister noted that was why my father was hanging on; he wanted his family to be together. About twenty minutes later, my father died, with my mother, my sister, my brother, and me beside him. I was hoping to have the full experience with my father, to be with him, accompany him across, and see the welcoming party receive him. But my own connection to the forces of this passage had been broken, and I could not get it back.

My mom and my siblings left soon after he died. I felt compelled to stay. I am not sure why, but I was feeling a lot of emotions, and I didn't want to cut short my experience of his death. I trusted that I would know when it was time for me to leave. So I sat at his bedside as my attention traveled through a vast array of sensations, emotions, and thoughts. I felt like a bystander as my inner world processed all that I was experiencing around the termination of this profound relationship. After about twenty-five minutes, I heard an unexpected knock on the door. Six of my father's longtime caregivers asked to come in. One by one, they approached him and surrounded his bed. They kissed him. They hugged him. It was so moving to see. They said how kind he was and how loving he was.

One woman, who was pregnant, told me how even with his dementia, he would put his hand on her stomach and say, "Baby, baby," and smile.

After they left, I stayed with my father's body, and I had a juxtaposition of emotions. I thought, "These people think you are so kind and so loving and so beautiful, and yet I never had that with you. Why couldn't we have had a better relationship?" And as I was thinking this, suddenly snippets of our life together came flooding back, scenes that I did not remember. They unfolded as if they were being given to me. Every scene was different visually, but energetically, each contained an emotional connection to or an emotional moment with my father, with my mother, or with my brother and sister. In one, we were on top of a mountain overlooking Lake Tahoe. My father was pleased with me; I had been attending graduate school at Harvard University. I remembered it and said to myself, *Oh my God. He did actually love me in that moment. I did feel that*. In these final moments with my father, I was receiving the experience of love and appreciation. And during this experience, I realized something deeply meaningful: that he'd done the best he could. My grandfather had died suddenly from a heart attack when my father was fourteen, and Dad never recovered from this loss.

Maybe this reconciliation came from my father, maybe from another loving force, but the experience was like an emotional life review, laying out the landscape of our father-son relationship. Sitting in that room, I was healing and grieving and emoting. I was bawling. And I could see things I hadn't appreciated before. The man who had just died was no longer merely my father, he was also a human being. And in seeing his humanness, I felt the fear he had felt as a father, I felt his challenges. But I saw them all differently. I didn't see them as rejection of me. I saw them as fear and desperation, and a need for my father to do his life's work of being a successful businessman, to fulfill what he perceived as the requirements to have proven himself a good son to his own father.

I may not have had the full SDE experience that I had hoped for, but I had the fuller SDE meaning. I do not know if my father chose me for this, or if it was orchestrated by someone else, even my grandfather. Perhaps he wanted to heal that relationship between my father and me because he knew that his early passing had been so harmful to his son. I know that I felt his deep gratitude to my mother and how much he really wanted to thank her. My mother met my father twenty months after his father's death, when she was fifteen and he was sixteen. They were never apart for sixty-four years.

Whatever its ultimate source, in that room I was overcome with a sense of healing. When I asked, "Help me understand this. How am I ever going to understand this relationship?" it's as if I was given the gift of a life review. A gift to me to understand my life with my father.

What brings you here?

Death is one of life's greatest mysteries. It defies our rational mind's need to know and desire to understand. Death remains shrouded, always just out of sight.

Yet I hope that having taken this journey to explore and understand shared death experiences, you will find yourself able to derive new and deeper meanings around the end of life. Recall Liz H.'s eloquent description of the lasting impact of her SDE with her son Nicolas. "In all the years since then, I have felt that there is something really wonderful and beautiful after this life. It's the most beautiful part of whatever your life is, was, or could have been." She adds, "I have this feeling that whatever comes next is actually a really beautiful gift."

I hope these stories from ordinary people just like you and me will provide solace for those of you who may fear death and inspiration for those of you who want to cross this great divide with confidence and courage. My lifetime of experiences and my scholarly research suggest that what awaits each of us at the end of this life is awesome, glorious, and loving, a reminder that there are gifts to be found at every stage of life, including its end. May you approach this great threshold with trust in the benevolence of an afterlife. I also hope this book will help guide you on your own path, to find new ways through grief, new opportunities for healing, and new meaning in the relationships you form. Above all, I hope that these stories will inspire you to fully embrace the wonder and great adventure of being human by living each moment with awe and gratitude for the gift of being alive.

May you find these gifts in your own life and the lives of those you love.

Appendix I:
The Shared Crossing Research Initiative

I'm frequently asked, How do you study shared death experiences? The answer is very much the way you would study any phenomenon: by gathering and analyzing data. I began the Shared Crossing Research Initiative (SCRI) in 2013 as a not-for-profit collaboration with the Family Therapy Institute of Santa Barbara. The mission of SCRI is to study a full range of end-of-life experiences and their therapeutic value for patients, their families, and caregivers. For more information on SCRI, go to SharedCrossing.com/research.

SCRI begins with a common definition of a shared death experience: *These are experiences that occur when an individual feels that they have somehow shared in a dying person's transition from this life to whatever lies beyond.* As you have by now discovered, a central theme found throughout shared death experiences is that of a journey: experiencers claim to sense, witness, accompany, and even guide the dying as they move toward some destination that nearly all reports depict as benevolent and beautiful.

Sir William Barrett was the first to collect and classify reports of what we now refer to as SDEs: in 1926, his book *Deathbed Visions*

introduced readers to the various experiences reported by caregivers and loved ones of the dying around the time of death. For
instance, he included the words of one man, a church dean, who
reported that while he and his wife were present at the deathbed
of their son, they both noticed "something rise as if it were from
his face like a delicate veil or mist, and slowly pass away . . . We
were deeply impressed and remarked, 'How wonderful! Surely,
that must be the departure of his spirit.'" More recently, Dr. Peter
Fenwick and Elizabeth Fenwick gathered stories of dozens of such
experiences occurring throughout the United Kingdom and Northern Europe. But it wasn't until 2011, with the publication of Dr.
Raymond Moody's book *Glimpses of Eternity*, that these experiences
acquired the name "shared death experiences." Before this, SDEs
were simply lumped together with a variety of other end-of-life
phenomena and were most often referred to as "deathbed visions."

SDEs are unique in that they suggest death may truly be an
interpersonal event—one that can be shared with loved ones in
some of the most extraordinary ways. Certainly not everyone has
an SDE at the time of death of a loved one. But among those who
do, their reports show that there are a number of consistent traits
within these experiences. SCRI has identified these traits by analyzing both written reports and transcripts from interviews that we
have conducted. SCRI confirmed two of my working hypotheses;
the first is that SDEs may occur either at the bedside or remotely,
and the second is that there are four distinct though not exclusive
ways in which people may experience an SDE: remotely sensing a
death, witnessing unusual phenomena attributed to a death, feelings of accompanying the dying, and feelings of assisting the dying.
Perhaps most important, SCRI found that SDEs leave an indelible

mark upon the people reporting them. These experiences seem to greatly influence what people believe, provide a healing context for grieving, and can even serve as catalysts for continued relational bonds with deceased loved ones.

Many of the interviews SCRI conducted highlighted both the difficulties and the therapeutic value of people openly discussing their experiences with health professionals. We learned that although SDEs can be deeply significant, sometimes individuals require help to process them. That disconnect has led us to wonder what extraordinary changes we might uncover if people felt completely free to discuss their experiences in a more supportive environment. We are hopeful, based on feedback from our published work in the *American Journal of Hospice and Palliative Medicine*, that receptivity to these experiences is growing. Indeed, this possibility helps drive our continued research and engagement.

Below, I have highlighted some of SCRI's key findings. More information can be found on our website and in our academic publications.

Key Findings

Surprisingly, the majority of SDEs that we studied—64 percent—were reported by individuals who were physically distant from the dying patient or loved one. Another interesting discovery was that more than 41 percent of the people whom we interviewed reported having more than one SDE. Our research confirmed that there are four distinct ways by which people may participate in an SDE. We refer to these as *Modes of Participation* and believe this typology is helpful to understand the full range of SDEs.

SDEs: Modes of Participation

SENSING   WITNESSING   ACCOMPANYING   ASSISTING

Experiencer	Experiencer	Experiencer	Experiencer
reports remotely	reports	reports	reports assisting
sensing the	witnessing	accompanying	(perhaps even
transition of the	phenomena	the dying as they	guiding) the
dying	associated with	transition	dying during
	the transition of		their transition
	the dying		

Remotely Sensing a Death

Remotely sensing a death occurred in nearly 21 percent of reports. Most often, people described having brief thoughts, feelings, and/ or a sense of the dying person's presence, usually at a time that is later determined to correspond with the moment of death. Many people also reported having received messages from the dying in which they imparted a final farewell. Less common were instances in which people reported the sudden onset of unusual physical symptoms, such as chest pains, drops in body temperature, and difficulty with breathing, which they believe corresponded to what their loved ones experienced as they died. In some instances, the living person made an immediate connection that a loved one had died; others made this connection only after learning of their loved one's death.

Witnessing Unusual Phenomena Attributed to a Death

The most commonly reported SDE consisted of the appearance of unusual phenomena, which was reported by more than 88 percent of the people we interviewed. The most frequent occurrence was a vision of the dying person (who typically appeared younger), followed by several less distinct visions: the appearance of a brilliant and transcendent light, a sensing of energies, perceived alterations in time and space, the appearance of nonhuman beings and entities, seeing what was believed to be the spirit leaving the body, the appearance or presence of previously deceased loved ones, and visions of otherworldly or heavenly realms. Less common were the appearance of tunnels or gateways and reports of "life reviews," during which people reported having witnessed past events in the lives of the dying.

Accompanying the Dying in a Visionary Realm

Slightly more than 15 percent of SDE reports included descriptions of having accompanied the dying person partway through their transition. According to these reports, participants suddenly found themselves out of body or in a completely different reality in the presence of the dying. People also reported that while undergoing this experience, they acquired special knowledge, which became inaccessible after they returned. A common feature in reports of accompanying the dying is an encounter with a border or boundary that people reported not being able or "permitted" to go beyond.

Assisting the Dying in Transitioning

About 9 percent of people described having taken an active role in assisting a loved one during the process of transitioning. These experiences were similar to those in which people accompanied the dying, but also included individuals who perceived that their attention, presence, and assistance were required by the dying to successfully transition.

Time of SDE Relative to Time of Death

Though most of the SDE accounts we analyzed occurred around the time of a death, more than 6 percent occurred hours to days before a death, and 14 percent occurred hours to days after a death. We noticed no substantive differences in features or effects related to the time of the SDE.

Major SDE Features and Their Prevalence

A Vision of the Dying Person	50%
Heightened Awareness/Expanded Knowledge	36%
Encounters with Nonliving Figures or Beings	29%
Transcendent Light	25%
Alterations in Perception of Linear Space/Time	18%
Seeing the Spirit Leave the Body	14%
Appearance of Heavenly Realms	12%
Boundary the Experiencer Cannot Cross	10%
Physical and Emotional Sensations	
Sensing Unusual Energy	42.6%
Overpowering Emotion	28%
Physical Sensations	8%

Changes in Beliefs, Attitudes, and Behavior

The aftermath of the SDE produced a number of quantifiable changes in the people we studied. Most noticeably, nearly 87 percent of those interviewed reported that their experience had left them absolutely convinced that there is a benevolent afterlife. More than 69 percent of those we interviewed said that their SDE had lessened or even removed their grief, and more than 52 percent of people that we interviewed said that their SDE had removed their fear regarding death and dying. In terms of religious or spiritual impact, over half of those interviewed self-identified as "spiritual, not religious," but 36 perecent reported that their SDE had led to them becoming "more spiritual."

We did come across a few people who had negative experiences attached to their SDEs. Five individuals experienced unaccounted-for physical symptoms and were initially fearful of the experience. However, most negative experiences reported were instances where people had shared their stories with others and had been dismissed or derided. Nearly 30 percent of those interviewed said that they wanted to talk about their experiences but were afraid of social ridicule or rejection. One highlight of our research interviews was that virtually every person we spoke with expressed a deep appreciation for the opportunity to share their experiences.

Finally, more than 24 percent of people reporting SDEs also said that they had maintained an ongoing relationship with their deceased loved one.

Conclusion

As we gather additional case studies, we continue to note the transformational effects of SDEs, the most prevalent being the conviction that the experience was objectively real and that it has revealed special knowledge: deceased loved ones are, in the words of one individual, "alive and well somewhere." We believe that a wider acknowledgment of these experiences offers significant potential for developing new approaches to end-of-life care for individuals and their loved ones.

If you have had a shared crossing and are interested in contributing your experience to our research, please go to SharedCrossing .com. Thank you for joining us in bringing the wisdom and healing of shared crossings to the world.

Appendix II: The Shared Crossing Project

I created the Shared Crossing Project (SCP) in order to raise awareness and educate people about the profound and healing experiences available to the dying and their loved ones. SCP offers a variety of programs, training materials, and presentations for the general public, health care providers, mental health professionals, and end-of-life practitioners.

The Shared Crossing Practitioner Certification Program is a comprehensive training that focuses on integrating the knowledge and application of shared crossings into a variety of clinical end-of-life and bereavement settings.

SCP also offers consulting and customized training to end-of-life and other community organizations. For more information, go to SharedCrossing.com.

SCP collects and studies shared crossings, so if you have had an extraordinary end-of-life experience, please go to SharedCrossing .com to learn how you can contribute your story to our research.

Acknowledgments

Thanks to Olivia and Lauren for their consistent support of my shared crossing work. Olivia often said it was "weird" explaining to her friends that her father studied death and the afterlife. Still, she and Lauren have cheered me on, putting up with the countless hours required to bring to life both the Shared Crossing Project and this book. I am grateful for their unwavering love.

Special thanks to my team of literary professionals, who assisted in birthing this book: Lyric Winik for her gift of transforming my ideas into eloquent words; Gail Ross, my literary agent, for her sage counsel at every step along the way; and Jon Tandler for his gentle and wise legal guidance.

Thanks to my stellar team at Simon & Schuster: my editor, Priscilla Painton, vice president and editorial director at Simon & Schuster, for her vision, guidance, and trust in our ability to write a meaningful and transformative book for a world in need of good news about death and dying; publisher Jonathan Karp for his vital support; Hana Park for her excellent and exceptionally helpful assistance; Sherry Wasserman in production; Jackie Seow for a beautiful cover design that truly captures the essence of this book; and Stephen Bedford and Elizabeth Herman, for their dedication to the best final product.

Thanks to Michael Kinsella, our chief of research, for his commitment to the Shared Crossing Project Mission of bringing the knowledge and transformation of shared crossings to those in search of a better relationship with death. His outstanding research skills assisted us in analyzing hundreds of stories that now serve as the seminal work in shared death studies. Many of these inspiring accounts appear in this book. Our friendship and collaboration as pioneers exploring the majesty of shared crossings has been a source of excitement and joy.

To Monica Williams, our medical director, for her courage and love of humanity that inspired her to challenge our health care system's relationship to death and dying. Her personal and professional experiences as an emergency department physician provided a valuable perspective on how our work could positively transform end-of-life care. I am grateful for her partnership in carrying this work to health care providers worldwide.

I am immensely grateful to our research participants, who courageously offered their stories, often sharing them for the first time. Their stories, drawn from the painful loss of a cherished loved one, illuminate the wonder and grandeur of the shared death experience.

To my colleagues at the Family Therapy Institute of Santa Barbara (FTI) for their encouragement to pursue the uncharted territories of the spiritual dimensions of death and dying. Special thanks to Debra Manchester, executive director, and Don MacMannis, clinical director, for their consistent support of the many facets of the Shared Crossing Project, in particular its Research Initiative and educational programs. Thanks to Deborah Harkin and Michael

Dunn for serving on the FTI Ethics Review Board, which provided guidance for our research. Thanks to Nancy Villalobos, FTI administrator, for her constant attention to my many requests.

I offer a well of gratitude to Thery Jenkins, who, as my associate, assisted in crafting and facilitating the first Shared Crossing Project Workshops. Her enthusiasm, impeccable group facilitation skills, and keen insight into the importance of these programs inspired me, as together we conducted our first research projects to study the impact on participants.

This book would not have come to fruition without my beloved Shared Crossing Community, which began with a committed group of Santa Barbarians who shared my vision to explore the great mystery of death and evolved into a movement dedicated to manifesting conscious, connected, and loving end-of-life experiences. Maribeth Goodman and Steve Knaub were founding members of our community and graciously offered their hearts and minds as we created the Shared Crossing Project Mission Statement and website. They were soon joined by Tom Craveiro and Liz Hogan, and the four of them together generously volunteered countless hours coordinating our first community events to raise awareness about shared crossings. Roger Himovitz, Arlene Stepputat, Judi Weisbart, Kate Carter, Barbara Bartolome, Leslee Goodman, Norman Risch, Sonja Linstrom, Victoria Harvey, Antoinette Chartier, Marianne Woodsome, Arlene Radasky, Barbara Wolfe, Claudia Crawford, Mimi deGruy, Sister Helen Wolkerstorfer, Toby Sternlieb, Nancy Shobe, Allison Armour, Barbara Morse, Nohl Martin, Nancy Shobe, Sonya Fairbanks, and Marsha Goldman, as well as others, stepped forward to offer valuable support as our movement grew. Each graciously shared their unique and valuable skills, including event planning and production, research assistance, community outreach, fundraising, document editing, video technical support, and more. A special thanks to Jennifer Parks and McDermott-Crockett Mortuary for the use of their sanctuary for many of our programs and to Hospice of Santa Barbara and VNA Health for welcoming our Shared Crossing Project perspective.

I am eternally grateful to Nancy Koppelman, who, before her untimely death, championed our work and brought multitudes of wonderful people to our programs and community. Nancy graciously hosted Shared Crossing Project events in her lovely seaside home, generously inviting her diverse array of friends to attend and participate in our gatherings.

As I look back now, these remarkable, like-minded people and organizations shared a common vision that made manifest what is now the Shared Crossing Project. Their support, counsel, and friendship continue to serve as constant reminders that our Shared Crossing Project Mission is essential in transforming our culture's relationship to death and dying. Their commitment to our mission also helped lay the groundwork for this book.

This book, the research, and all that the Shared Crossing Project has developed would not have been possible without the hard work and dedication of our SCP staff. A warm appreciation to Noel Christensen and Michelle Johnston, our staff researchers, who have worked tirelessly analyzing hundreds of interviews; big thanks to our three SCP & SCRI research administrators, Kattie Bachar, Laurel Huston, and Kelly Rose Almeida, who provided excellent help and support during this book process; additionally, a huge thank-you to Amanda Lake, Sierra Boatwright, Linx Latham, Jessica Pepper, and Sarita Relis, SCP administrators who paved the road that has brought us to this book. A special thanks to Robert Fortune for his brilliant technical support, Joy Margolis for her insightful consulting, and Kim Sutherland for her skillful bookkeeping. Thanks to Maribeth Goodman, Katie Karas, and Noel Christensen for also sensitively critiquing the manuscripts.

A heartfelt thank-you to Raymond Moody, Lisa Smartt, Maggie Callanan, Eben Alexander, and Karen Newell, who offered essential support, guidance, and friendship in the creation of this book.

I am grateful to Jan Holden, Pim van Lommel, Bruce Greyson, and Peter Fenwick for their wise counsel, thoughtful review, and sincere encouragement regarding the research work of the Shared Crossing Research Initiative, which provided the findings that fill this book.

A warm appreciation to Marge Cafarelli, with whom I share a long and trusted friendship, for her wise counsel regarding the growth and development of the SCP. Thanks to my longtime friend, Jeremiah Marshman, with whom I have shared a bounty of insightful conversations, which have supported me in the writing of this book. And, with thanks to my friend Ken Saxon, whose Courage to Lead program assisted me in staying balanced to wholeheartedly pursue the Shared Crossing Project Mission.

To Robert Hall, Al Miller, and Leo Rock, who served as wise mentors and trusted friends before they left their human lives. They continue to inspire me, and I think of them often as I carry out our mission.

Shared Crossing Research Initiative's Partners and Supporters

Our pioneering Shared Crossing Research Initiative, which revealed these profound stories, was made possible by the generous support of our compassionate, wise, and truly forward-thinking partners. They understood and embraced our mission to bring these powerful stories to the world. They encouraged me, believing that these stories would transform end-of-life care for the dying and their loved ones, as well as the health care systems that serve them. Thank you!

With deep appreciation to Jennifer and Peter Buffett and to the James S. Bower Foundation, Jon Clark, and Harvey Bottelsen.

Special thanks to Carrie Cooper and Rhino Griffith, Natalie Fleet-Orfalea and Lou Buglioli, Linda and Fred Gluck, Deborah Gunther, Patricia Selbert, Richelle and Omar Gaspar, and Melbourne Smith.

Thanks as well to Arlene and Dr. William Radasky, Sandra Tyler, Stacy and Ron Pulice, Marge Cafarelli and Jan Hill, Jill and Barry Kitnick, Katie Karas, and Sharon Felder.

Finally, thanks to you, the reader, for your time and interest. It is my sincere hope that this book can be of help to you at any stage of life.

About the Authors

WILLIAM PETERS, M.Ed, MFT, is the founder of the Shared Crossing Project and director of its Research Initiative. Recognized as a global leader in the field of shared death studies, he has spent decades studying end-of-life experiences. Previously, Peters worked as a hospice volunteer with the Zen Hospice Project in San Francisco and as a teacher and social worker in Central and South America. A practicing psychotherapist, he holds degrees from Harvard University's Graduate School of Education and University of California, Berkeley. His work on the end of life is informed by his therapeutic work with individuals and families facing grief and bereavement, personal experiences with death and dying across cultures, and his family's own end-of-life journeys. See more at www .SharedCrossingProject.com.

MICHAEL KINSELLA, PH.D, is chief of research for the Shared Crossing Research Initiative. His work on spirituality and end-of-life experiences has appeared in multiple scholarly books and journals.